PORTFOLIO INDEXING

OTHER TITLES IN THE WILEY FRONTIERS IN FINANCE SERIES

Options, Futures and Exotic Derivatives
Eric Briys, Mondher Bellalah, Huu Minh Mai and François de Varenne

Buying and Selling Volatility
Kevin B. Connolly

Beyond Value at Risk
Kevin Dowd

Investment Valuation
Ashwath Damodaran

Project Financing
John D. Finnerty

Valuation
Tom Copeland, Tim Koller, and Jack Murrin

PORTFOLIO INDEXING

Theory and Practice

Harold Hutchinson

JOHN WILEY & SONS, LTD

Chichester · New York · Weinheim · Brisbane · Singapore · Toronto

Baffins Lane, Chichester,
West Sussex PO19 1UD, England

National 01243 779777
International (+ 44) 1243 779777
e-mail (for orders and customer service enquiries): cs-books@wiley.co.uk
Visit our Home Page on http://www.wiley.co.uk
or http://www.wiley.com

Other Wiley Editorial Offices

John Wiley & Sons, Inc., 605 Third Avenue,
New York, NY 10158–0012, USA

WILEY-VCH Verlag GmbH, Pappelallee 3,
D-69469 Weinheim, Germany

Jacaranda Wiley Ltd, 33 Park Road, Milton,
Queensland 4064, Australia

John Wiley & Sons (Asia) Pte Ltd, 2 Clementi Loop #02–01,
Jin Xing Distripark, Singapore 129809

John Wiley & Sons (Canada) Ltd, 22 Worcester Road,
Rexdale, Ontario M9W 1L1, Canada

Library of Congress Cataloging-in-Publication Data

Hutchinson, Harold.
Portfolio indexing: theory and practice/Harold Hutchinson.
p. cm.—(Wiley frontiers in finance)
Includes bibliographical references and index.
ISBN 0–471–98868–5 (alk. paper)
1. Portfolio management—Mathematical models. 2. Capital assets pricing model. I. Title. II. Series.
HG4529.5.H88 1999
332.6—dc21 99–20545
CIP

British Library Cataloguing in Publication Data

A catalogue record for this book is available from the British Library

ISBN 0-471-98868-5

Typeset in 12/14pt Times by Vision Typesetting, Manchester
Printed and bound in Great Britain by Biddles Ltd, Guildford and King's Lynn
This book is printed on acid-free paper responsibly manufactured from sustainable forestry, in which at least two trees are planted for each one used for paper production.

Contents

To my Mother, Father, and brother Peter,

and to

Elena, Pablo and Andres

in the greatest part of our Concernment
God has afforded only the Twilight,
As I may say so, of Probability,
suitable to that state of Mediocrity and Probationership
He has been pleased to place us in here.

John Locke (1632–1704)

Foreword

ROD CROSS

Professor of Economics, ICMM, University of Strathclyde

Since the 1970s the plausible argument that, in certain circumstances, free markets work best has hardened into the dogma that free markets always operate in a benign way. The counterpart to this doctrine in financial markets is the efficient markets hypothesis, which applies arbitrage conditions to deduce the implications that financial markets process information efficiently and price risk appropriately. The related CAPM model suggests that investment managers should be replaced by automatic pilots, who follow Noah in taking all the security species into their investment arks, weighting the securities by their importance in some super-index of world security life forms, and borrowing or lending in some safe security to achieve the desired level of overall risk.

Doubts about the empirical validity of the CAPM model have arisen in relation to the pricing of individual securities, weekend and January effects on stock market returns, and the basic problem that indices cover some things rather than everything. In *Portfolio Indexing* Harold Hutchinson unravels the foundations underlying the CAPM—indexed portfolio orthodoxy. The presence of informational deficiencies and asymmetries mean that financial markets are afflicted by adverse selection and moral hazard problems. In this world investors are guessing about the beliefs held by, and the information available to, other investors: market prices are driven in good part by such webs of belief. It is a world of strategic interaction in which timing is important, and in which the securities selected for investment arks might have to be ditched in stormy seas lest the arks sink. Investment strategies are not a matter of indexed rules but of discretionary management.

When sailing on a buoyant sea of bull markets there is little reason to doubt the prevailing wisdom about how financial markets work: it is difficult not to make money, even with a misguided investment strategy; and imprudent bank lending can be rolled over on the back of rising asset prices. Once the waves of pessimism rise, and fears of shipwreck and recession surface, the time to re-examine the conventional wisdom comes. In fact the much-publicised financial crises of 1997–98 are merely the tip of an iceberg which, according to the IMF, has encompassed three-quarters of its member countries at various times since the late 1970s. So the appearance of the present book is timely indeed.

The exposition is a masterpiecc. Otherwise difficult concepts are explained in a simple, intuitive way but without loss of rigour, and are illuminated by the author's firsthand knowledge of how financial markets work. *Portfolio Indexing* does for financial markets what *Zen and the Art of Motorcycle Maintenance* did for natural philosophy. The recommended portfolio maintenance strategy involves using an early warning system to exclude markets and securities that are prone to crash. Professionals, students and amateur investors alike will profit from this enjoyable tract on how to maintain and navigate vehicles of investment.

Preface

The dominant paradigm in modern-day fund management remains the Capital Asset Pricing Model (CAPM). Originally developed in the 1960s as an explanatory and predictive model of capital market behaviour, it has subsequently acquired enormous normative significance in many fund-management institutions (this is not just how capital markets behave but how fund management, or more accurately non-management, should be practised). I say non-management because the fact is that the overriding conclusion of CAPM is that passive market indexing is the best combination of risk and return available for equity investors. If you want more risk than that offered by the market itself, you should simply gear up, borrowing funds to buy more of the market portfolio; if you want less risk than the market, you should switch part of your portfolio into 'riskless' Treasury Bills.

CAPM potentially goes much further than the better-known Efficient Markets Hypothesis (EMH) which basically says that since everything to be known about a company is already imbedded in the price of that company's share, an active trading investment policy cannot beat an inactive one. However EMH does not necessarily imply portfolio indexing as an optimal strategy, but rather a passive approach to investment management where the chosen portfolio, which may or may not be the market portfolio, is tailored to the individual's appetite for risk. With CAPM however, even this degree of tailoring is unnecessary. There is only one portfolio (the full market index) which it makes sense for everyone to hold. It is as simple as that. 'Stock picking', 'strategic' or 'tactical' asset allocation, and even 'tailor-made' passive portfolios other than the market index are all out! Buy the market portfolio, cut your broker commissions and sleep easy at night in the knowledge that you are holding the best portfolio available—what could be easier or better than that!

Intuitively at least, the approach appears to have its attractions. Despite their deservedly august reputation, as recently as 1997, the four largest active pension fund management houses in the UK failed to match the returns on the UK All Share Index over that year. Mercury Asset Management's pooled vehicle achieved an annual return of 14.6%, PDFM's 20.7%, Schroders 19.1% and Gartmore's 17.0%, against a 1997 All Share Index return of 23.6%. In the US in 1997, a paltry 10% of all actively managed funds, pension or otherwise, managed to beat the index. Such evidence may seem to be strong support for an indexing approach to fund management, especially given the undoubted but at times costly talent employed by the active investment houses with the specific objective of beating the market hurdle.

However, intuition can be a valued friend or a dangerous guide. A little more thought reveals that there have been a host of famous investment gurus over the years including Benjamin Graham, Warren Buffett, T. Rowe Price, John Templeton, and George Soros, to mention but a few of the better-known names, who despite the occasional gaffe or bout of under-performance, seem to have records suggesting that you can, in fact, consistently 'beat the market' with an active investment style over the long term. Even the distinguished economist Paul Samuelson, a supposed sceptic of the active fund management approach, was reputedly an investor in Buffett's investment company, Berkshire Hathaway, an example in the world of finance, perhaps, of Pascal's wager. Nevertheless, with currently an estimated 35% or more of all institutional funds under management in the US indexed (20% in the UK)—with the relevant percentages even higher if one looks only at the pension fund segment of the market—and a good deal of what remains 'quasi-indexed', that is index funds in disguise where the actual portfolio weightings are tilted only marginally away from the index weightings, it is clear that there is a large and still growing body of opinion opposed not just to active fund management techniques, but also favourably disposed to the indexing alternative.

The outline of this book is to give the reader the necessary conceptual background to understand the indexing debate (Chapter 1). Most of this material emerged in the post-Second World War era and was subsequently crystallised in CAPM (Chapter 2), the cornerstone of modern finance theory and the most powerful theoretical argument in favour of passive portfolio indexing. Chapter 3 scrutinises the foundations of CAPM and finds it flawed, most importantly in failing to address the informational asymmetries and deficiencies that characterise financial markets, as well as ignoring the strategic intrigue between market participants which is at the heart of capital market dynamics. When one seriously examines these issues, and their consequences for stocks and markets, the dangers of tying one's fortune to the Ouija board of various stock market indices, rather than the advantages of a passive fund management approach, start to become all too evident.

In Chapter 4, I discuss what I believe to be a more reasonable alternative to market indexing in the 'complex' financial markets of today. The approach replaces the deductive reasoning of CAPM with a less-ambitious but arguably more realistic inductive approach to the investment problem. To some extent I turn the investment question on its head—rather than asking what stocks to hold in a portfolio, I suggest a better starting point for the portfolio manager is to ask what stocks not to hold in a portfolio. I examine and recommend filter mechanisms for avoiding stocks and markets which are substantially overvalued and liable to 'crash' corrections. Early Warning Systems have an important role to play in stock selection and market strategy, yet remain largely in their infancy in most fund management institutions. On the positive side, I look at tentative strategies for investing in what I think is best described as the twilight—that is financial markets which are at times confused and confusing, and where our knowledge is at best imperfect. I specifically address to what extent investments need to be diversified *à la* CAPM in such a world.

Are these issues ultimately important? I think so. An impressionable general public is now subjected to a daily barrage of advertisements in the press on just how to invest their savings. With pension provision in many developed and developing countries moving increasingly into the domain of the private sector, and with mutual funds and other equity products increasingly being viewed by the public as alternative investment vehicles to the more traditional fixed-interest banking products, the need to understand the financial markets has gained importance for the ordinary citizen. Meanwhile, governments encourage us to invest in privatisations in companies, some of which at least that were originally nationalised having lost any apparent hope of ever making a profit! Like it or not, we have all become players in the financial arena which at times can have the appearance more of a circus arena than of anything else. And to borrow a phrase from a well-known poem about the circus by that unrivalled examiner of the lost enchantments of the Celtic twilight, the Irish poet W.B. Yeats, we do not wish to become mesmerised, with the 'players and painted stage' taking all our attention at the expense of deeper truths. It is an arena we must try to understand, or at least to know what are the limits of our understanding.

Often the adverts aim to make it look all too easy with the underlying reality cloaked behind marketing gimmicks. In particular, portfolio indexing is often heralded as the way ahead in investment management. I consider the argument in favour of portfolio indexing to be on a par with the argument that we should conduct our lives by reading the star maps. Nevertheless, portfolio indexing is increasingly accepted by both industry practitioners and by their regulators as the optimal way to manage money. No wonder the crowds are inclined to follow. I hope this book encourages you to think twice about following the crowd, and about letting the players and painted stage distort the underlying reality.

While this book is written for professional investors and students on finance courses, I have constructed it in a way that will hopefully make it useful to general readers with an interest in investment, on the grounds that, as I have said, I believe the issue of indexing is of relevance to a wide public. This has entailed a certain amount more geometry and more prose at the expense of pure mathematics than some specialists (and certainly some of my academic friends!) might have liked. This is not to decry the mathematical method *per se* which for the specialist remains the purest and most concise way to develop arguments in finance. However, such purity comes at the cost of excluding many interested generalists. This is unfortunate as such people have from their own insights and experience much to add to the debate. I have also 'boxed' parts of the text. Some boxes contain additional material designed to give food for thought on the issues raised in this book to both the professional and layperson alike. Other boxes contain more technical material that can be skipped at a first reading. Finally, to ease the burden, I have chosen a narrative style for parts of the text, with its hero Tom, a young fund manager trying to make sense of it all. The inspiration for Tom was Paul Simon's magnificent song 'The only living boy in New York', a song which I mention in the text and which I think any budding investment professional should listen to carefully. Like Tom, all other characters are fictitious.

Acknowledgements

My own interest in fund management issues in general, and in particular in the value of indexing portfolios as a portfolio strategy, followed from various events. My years at St. Andrews University, first as student and subsequently as lecturer, afforded me the opportunity to meet some marvellous people who introduced me to the crucial issue of methodology in economics (here I owe a special debt to Professor Rod Cross now at the University of Strathclyde). My graduate years as student at St. Antony's College, University of Oxford, and subsequently as college lecturer at Hertford College, gave me a unique and privileged chance to begin to come to grips with the wonders of microeconomics as applied to financial markets with Professor George Yarrow patiently expounding the theory. The chance to lecture on these subjects myself for several years undoubtedly helped to enliven and hopefully deepen my understanding of the subject matter—I certainly owe more to my students of those days and to my fellow lecturer and research collaborator, Dr. Andrew Allan (now at Salomon Brothers Smith Barney) than they do to me.

Then came the chance to see it all at first hand both as stockbroker and fund manager. Particular thanks must go to colleagues at European Stockbroker Carnegie International for having been prepared to take the risk in employing an academic to give advice to a colourful and dynamic sales force that believed economics (and economists!) were both best kept to the lecture theatre, and to the fund managers over my years who took the time to listen to my ideas or who impressed me with their particular fund-management style. Without committing them in any way to the ideas of this book, I owe a special debt to Mark Edwards at T. Rowe Price Fleming, Rupert Tate at Mercury Asset Management, Ken Baksh at Legal and General, Dexter Bree, formerly at Hill Samuel Asset Management, Patrick Vermeulen at Schroders Investment Management, James MacMillan at Merill Lynch Asset Management, Scott Jaffrey from Pictet, Dean Smith at TT International, Richard Webb and Steve Bates at Flemings Investment Management, Murdo Murchison at Templeton, Des Sullivan at Bank of Ireland Pension Fund, Serge Selfslaugh at Santander Partners, John Legat formerly at LGT, Richard Bruce at GLG Partners, John Armitage at Egerton, Stuart Mitchell at Morgan Grenfell Investment Management, Kieran Gallagher at Newton Investment Management, Tony Nutt and Richard Pease at Jupiter Investment Management, Malcolm MacDonald at NPI, and Phillip Keane at IBJ International. From all these people I have had insight into how good fund managers operate in complex markets. Finally I am indebted to the Hon. Kevin Packenham, Chairman of John Govett, for affording me the opportunity to take a hard look at the Mexican economy after the 1994 economic and stock market reversal (a subject I examine in some detail later in the book), to Francis Clarke and Peter Fernandez (both at Flemings) and to the Hon. Christopher Littleton, Chris Munro and above all James Buchanan Jardine (all from NCL) for the support they gave me during the time I advised the River and Mercantile Latin American Fund.

Thanks must also go to some true friends I have had the privilege to know over the years. Barry Adams, Miguel Trigo (tragically no longer with us), Jose Cerezo, Enrique Perez Pla, Mark Giacopazzi, Magnus Mathewson, Peter Tennyson, Rob Bell, Alan Martin and Glenn Coltart have all been helpful in thinking about the issues raised in this book and have had the kindness to buy me a Guinness at the same time. Current London work colleagues Jonathan Gosling, Ylwa Warghusen, Chris Hudson, Marcus Edwards Jones and Nigel Lloyd have added similar value during the twilight hours, as have all of the magnificent Credit Lyonnais team in Madrid. From Maria Luz Ruano and her brother Pedro I have enjoyed an insight into Colombian and Latin American financial life that otherwise would have escaped me. I would like to thank the management at Credit Lyonnais Securities Europe and Laing and Cruickshank Investment Management for all their help and encouragement, and in particular to Michael Kerr-Dineen, Michèle Jardin, John Davies, Paul Wright, Angela Whelan, Pierre Walter and Rafael Sarandeses for permitting and encouraging me to take the time to complete the script. Without the last-minute assistance of Paula Machin, Jackie Mann and Natalie Chemin, this book would never have made it to press on time. Thanks are also due to the editors at my publishers, John Wiley and Sons Ltd.

Thanks also to three true family friends, Jorge Nuñez Lasso de la Vega, Ana Nuñez Alvarez, and Ignacio Alvarez Carlon for unwavering support and for help in writing the sections on the machinations of the Spanish stock market in the late 1980s and early 1990s. Above all thanks to my wife Elena for having put up with me during the writing and for having kept the 'young terrors' as far away from the computer as possible. Obviously neither she, nor anyone else mentioned here, bears any blame for faults in my analysis or for vagueness in my thinking. These short-comings are, alas, very definitely my own.

1

A Random Walk Through Finance Theory—Essential Building Blocks

INTRODUCTION—THE MYSTERY OF INVESTMENT

Portfolio investment is a mysterious subject, continually confronting us with the unexpected and challenging the intellect to look for explanations. Here is just one David-versus-Goliath-type example. The latter half of the Victorian age saw a wave of investment from London, the global financial capital of that era, into Latin America. At the forefront of this investment was a set of UK investment houses, some of which are still around, such as the distinguished house of Scottish Widows, others of which have now disappeared into oblivion such as the once-magnificent River Plate Trust Loan and Agency Company, and still others that seem to be able to survive one way or another whatever the disasters met on the way, including the great house of Barings which is where this particular story begins.

Barings was one of the primary UK banking houses financing the development of Latin America in the last quarter of the nineteenth century. However, in that era as today, competition was intense for the lucrative deals available in emerging markets, especially in the financing of new infrastructure. One of Barings' competitors in the Southern cone of Latin America was the aggressive little River Plate Trust Loan and Agency Company, a London-based investment fund. This company had nothing like the capital resources of the much larger and better-known Barings—in fact the poor Trust company's shareholders were always wrangling about how to raise fresh money—but this did not stop the fund bidding for and winning some big deals in South America. The Trust's biggest coup was purchasing and restructuring the Montevideo waterworks on the northern side of the River Plate. The stake was sold some years later for a considerable profit.

Barings was not about to be ruffled by the coup and determined to make amends on the southern bank of the Plate. Alas, things did not work out so well. In 1888, Barings had to bail out the Argentine Government with acceptance credits when a several million pounds issue of stock in the Buenos Aires Waterworks company failed to find investors, thus precluding the famous 1890 Barings crisis. That time at least Barings was bailed out by the public sector in the guise of the Bank of England. When the cap was passed around again over one hundred years later, things did not prove so easy!

That, in a nutshell, is the mystery of investment. One small finance house buys a waterworks company, restructures it, and sells out at a profit. Simultaneously, on the other side of the river, so to speak, a large finance house takes an interest in an apparently very similar investment, cannot find anyone to back the idea, and almost goes bust as a result. Explain that! How can one possibly hope to give proper investment advice when the investment universe itself is so devilish?

Like it or not, the jobs of the investment analyst and fund manager are to do just that. 'Fair is foul and foul is fair' was an apt forewarning from the three witches of the mysteries and paradoxes in Macbeth's kingdom. A similar warning is an appropriate starting point for anyone seriously wanting to come to grips with the investment world. The fundamental issue is this. Despite the uncomfortable uncertainty of Macbeth's world, ultimately it was predictable with the tragic-hero's fatal flaw driving the story to an inevitable if unpleasant climax. Not all uncertainty shares this predictability. In fact one major strand in finance thought has it that investment is no more than a lottery governed solely by the calculus of chance and probability. In such a world, all we can know are the odds, nothing more than that. Other theorists doubt that we can know even this, with a veil of vagueness and uncertainty shrouding any predictability either deterministic or probabilistic.

For better or worse, these various investment theories are largely couched in terms of forbidding formulas in unfamiliar symbolic notation. For the average reader, these mathematical constructions tend to range from the very difficult to understand to the completely impossible to understand! Trying to wade through a few pages of many graduate finance textbooks in a crowded tube or while the baby is screaming in the bath is a sure recipe for confusion, or at least a trip back to the bookshop for the undergraduate version. Thankfully all is not lost. Most of the key concepts in these models are quite straightforward to understand with the help of a few graphs and just a little thought. Readers can take some comfort from the reply given by one of the outstanding finance theorists of the century, Professor James Tobin, who when asked to explain as simply as possible the conclusions of his work on portfolio choice, replied that his work showed that it was not sensible to put all one's eggs in the same basket!

This book then is about finding, if possible, rational or at least reasonable principles to guide decisions made by portfolio investors, and in particular whether passive portfolio indexing emerges as the winning rule to guide portfolio choice. Portfolio indexing embraces Tobin's old wives' tale, encouraging us to spread our risk, but as we shall see, it goes much further than that. In effect indexing tells us to invest in all marketable securities in proportion to their market capitalisation. Spreading risk through indexing may sound intuitive enough, but sometimes it pays to be wary of intuition and old wives' tales, as the witches' 'fair is foul and foul is fair' refrain reminds us.

So then, just how should we construct an optimal investment portfolio? Think of building a portfolio as being like packing a set of clothes before setting out on a holiday. This image seems particularly apt given that the Latin root of 'investment' (vestis) in fact means just that—clothing. Then the individual items of clothing we pack are simply the various financial and real assets in which we can invest today, including cash and Treasury bills, private-company bonds and shares, gold and other precious metals, pictures and antiques etc. We know that as we set off on a summer holiday that it will not in general be optimal to pack a suitcase-full of winter clothes (unless we are going to Scotland that is!) and similarly when we set of for a skiing weekend, it would not usually be sensible to pack only a swimming suit. In each case there is a variable that we cannot control (the weather) which can bring pleasant or unpleasant surprises, but also a variable that we can control (the clothes we pack). What we do is to try to tailor the variable we do control to meet our reasonable expectations of what might confront us because of the variable we do not control, in particular the actual weather conditions we shall face. How then should we pack our financial suitcases to best allow us to transfer wealth from one year to the next? Again there is a variable we can control (the assets we buy) but a variable over which we have no control (the economic environment in the future). The problem, as we shall see, is that preparing an optimal portfolio is not quite as easy as preparing for that holiday.

While there is near-uniform agreement amongst investment specialists that some form of diversification (that is financial jargon for not putting all one's eggs in the same basket) is desirable, there is not much general agreement on anything else. Even if we confine ourselves to the issue of what financial assets to hold as opposed to the wider question of combining 'real' assets (such as a house or a diamond ring) and 'paper' assets (such as bonds and shares), wide differences of viewpoint exist. What we can say is that 'active' professional investors, that is those who do not simply look to purchase a set of shares and leave it idle, nor to buy an equity index fund, essentially approach portfolio construction from one of two standpoints. A first route, usually referred to as the 'stock picking' or the 'bottom up' approach, suggests that it is less important to have the proportions of the different types of assets in a portfolio 'right' than to find the 'right' individual assets (especially the debt and equity instruments of private-sector companies). In this context 'right' is usually interpreted to mean giving the greatest return to the investor, given that investor's particular risk characteristics (see Box 1.1).

Box 1.1 Stockpicking—The Magnifying Glass and the Crystal Ball

Stock pickers usually start from the position that stock markets are whimsical and often driven away from fair value by professional intermediaries who have little idea of the true underlying characteristics of the companies concerned. That gives the stock picker the opportunity to buy and sell when markets are misaligned, so long as the stock picker really knows the underlying companies. Stock pickers themselves naturally divide into those who look at companies 'through a magnifying glass' and those that look at companies 'through a crystal ball'. The former scrutinise available public information to find hidden clues about a company's true worth; the latter try to forecast a company's prospects by looking beyond the immediate situation it faces.

Perhaps the most famous investor in the former category was Benjamin Graham. Sceptical of forecasting on the grounds of the inevitably subjective inputs into forecasting models, Graham instead concentrated on what was already known about companies. One stock picking technique pioneered by Graham and still used in some investment houses was to focus on the balance sheet status of companies regardless of their profitability and management. In a balance sheet sense, the value of a company's equity is the sum of its fixed and net current assets, minus its debt. The investment rule was to buy a portfolio of stocks whose market capitalisation was less than the value of net current assets minus all debt liabilities. Obviously an investor who can find such companies is in effect buying the fixed assets for free. To quote Graham 'we used this approach extensively in managing investment funds and over a thirty-odd-year period we must have earned an average of some 20% per annum from this source'.

Within the alternative forward-looking approach to stock picking, one of the great names is T. Rowe Price. He emphasised a mixed quantitative and qualitative approach to selecting stocks, rather than the pure quantitative balance sheet appraisal of Graham. Price's basic idea was to identify 'growth' industries and then to focus on promising companies (in terms of earnings per share growth) within the industry, the earlier in their life cycle the better. The secret was then to buy these companies in periods of market weakness and to hold these companies for a long period of time. Requirements for growth status included such things as superior management or Research and Development within the company, preferably operating in a relatively unregulated or uncompetitive market. Price was aware that any of the factors which gave a company a competitive advantage such as superior research could change dramatically and hence so too could the company's growth prospects. Hence with Price there was a quantitative aspect as well, with particular vigilance in terms of watching a company's evolution including its earnings and management record, things cast to one side in Graham's approach.

Table 1.1 Example of an Asset Allocation Approach

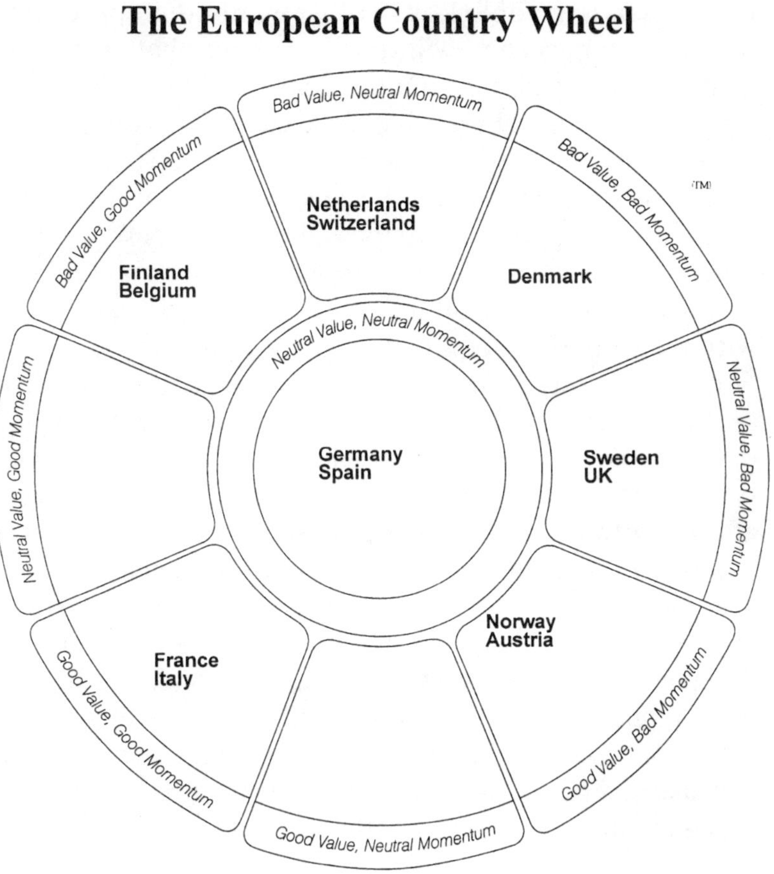

Credit Lyonnais Securities Europe regularly produces a 'strategy wheel' designed to guide investors to attractive sectors and markets, in terms of both 'value' and 'momentum'. In this chart we show an example of the European country wheel as at October 1998. Interestingly the approach can also be used from a 'bottom up' perspective to identify stock ideas.

Source: Credit Lyonnais Securities Europe.

The second route is the so-called 'asset allocation' or 'top down' approach to portfolio management. This method is much more concerned with finding the right proportions in which to hold the different asset classes comprising a portfolio rather than looking for individually splendid stocks or other assets (see Table 1.1). In other words, this approach to portfolio management will start by asking what proportion of stocks versus bonds an individual should hold in a portfolio rather than asking whether Microsoft is going to outperform the US market over the coming twelve months or other relevant time period. Because this approach looks at broad groupings of assets (stocks, bonds, property etc.) it is much more concerned with the workings of markets, and with what dictates or influences market trends, rather than with the valuation of individual assets in themselves.

Unfortunately in my view, these two schools are often seen as polar opposites, whereas I hope to show by the end of this book that they share much in common. In particular, both stock picking and active asset allocation are radically at odds with the alternative approach to investment, that is passive portfolio indexing. But that is to anticipate. Whichever view one espouses, any serious enquiry into portfolio choice must start with an understanding of how prices of financial instruments such as stocks and bonds are actually determined on markets. As we shall see, this will give us a vital introductory clue on just how to pack that financial suitcase and hence how to begin to deal with the mysteries and uncertainties of the investment world.

HOW FINANCIAL MARKETS WORK

To begin to understand just how difficult portfolio choice actually is, think of the institutional arrangements under which stocks, bonds, commodities, financial futures and options etc. are actually priced on markets. We are all used to seeing the volatility of these prices daily on our TV screens and in the press, and we probably all remember vaguely the idea of demand and supply determining prices, but what is actually going on day and night in the financial marketplace?

The fact is that these asset prices are not determined in the short run by the current demand and supplies for the asset brought to the market (demand and supply are flow concepts meaning by this a certain amount of the commodity per year or per month or per day etc.), but rather by the willingness of specialist intermediary traders to hold existing stocks of the asset in question. Daily equilibrium in a financial market is a stock concept, not a flow concept. The willingness of these traders to hold stocks determines the current market price, which in turn determines the flow demands and supplies that come to the market in the longer term.

To see how stock concepts can swamp flow concepts we need look no further than the determination of the gold price. By 1996, the gap between the conventional supply of gold (newly-mined metal and scrap) and demand for gold had reached about 700 tonnes (demand in excess of supply), a trend that had been increasing for several years. Why did the first half of the 1990s not then witness an enormous gold run (Figure 1.1)? The answer is that stocks of gold—not including the estimated 36 000 tonnes held by Central Banks and other financial institutions at that time—totalled about 85 000 tonnes. Threats of even small movements in such huge stocks can clearly override annual flow considerations. Admittedly some of these stocks are held as jewellery. However, in case you thought a gold ring was for ever, you might like to ponder on the thought that in 1993 alone, over 500 tonnes of melted-down jewellery came out of the Middle East from specialist traders in response to an increase in the gold price. Everlasting love!

What determines these prices at which the specialist trader is prepared to hold stocks without swamping the market? Presumably the specialist is concerned to try to make a short-term profit on his holding. Hence the price of any asset as quoted on a daily basis by the specialist depends on his expectation concerning the price of that asset or commodity tomorrow and the next day and the next *ad infinitum.*

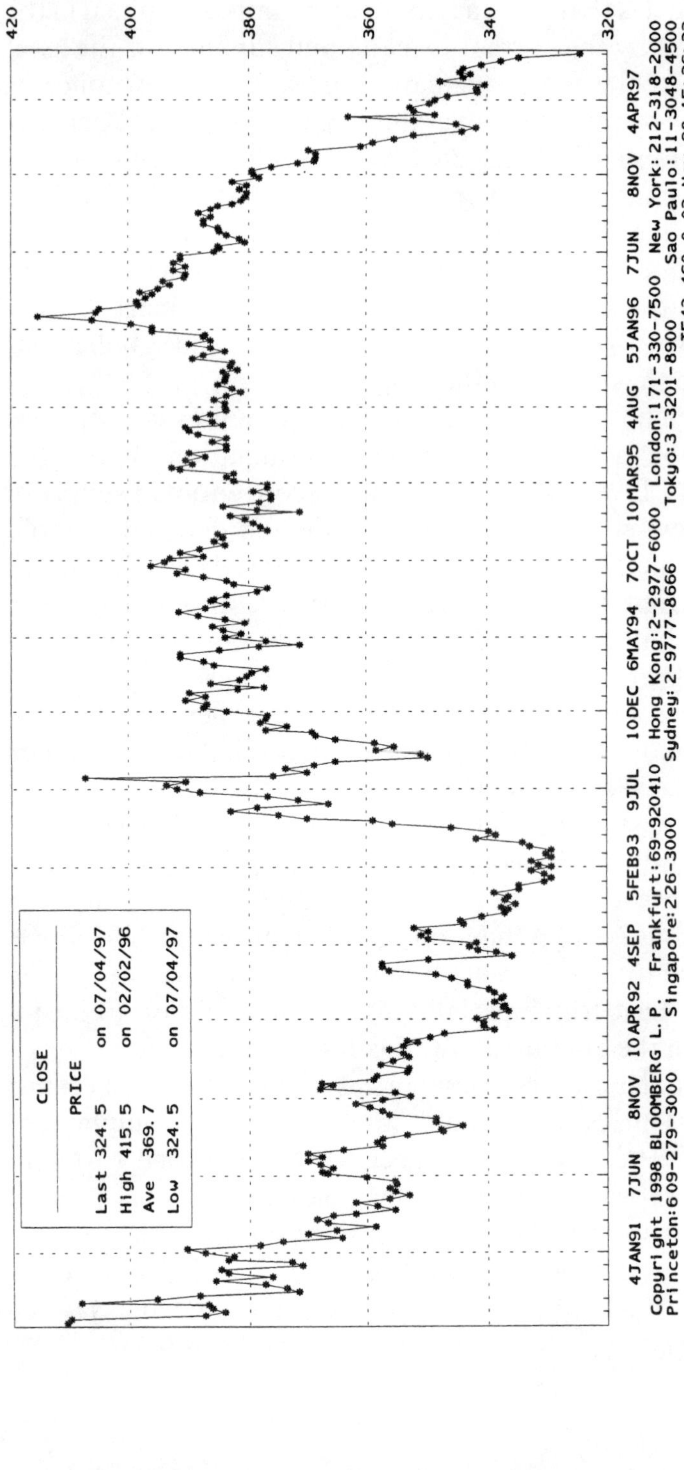

Figure 1.1 The Gold Price August 1990–April 1997

Source: Bloomberg

Think again of the gold price. Gold, unlike most shares and bonds, pays no dividend or fixed interest—the return comes entirely through the capital gain or loss. Today's expected capital gains will depend on the estimated price of gold tomorrow. But this in turn depends on the expected capital gain to be enjoyed from buying gold tomorrow and hence on the price of gold the day after tomorrow etc. Such expectations pyramids pervade all financial asset markets to a greater or lesser degree, with ever-more-shaky expectations stretching indefinitely into the future. This is our vital introductory clue as to the nature of the pricing of financial assets. But how then can we possibly hope to put together portfolios of these assets given these expectations pyramids, without divine-like revelation of how the whole future of the world will actually turn out? Without this, on what foundations do we build our expectations of future events?

That is the aim of modern portfolio theory, examined in Chapter 2. This approach to financial decision making under uncertainty is built on four crucial concepts, namely:

1. Subjective probability theory associated particularly with the name of Professor Leonard Savage.
2. The formalisation of uncertainty as risk, developed principally by Professors Kenneth Arrow and John Von Neumann.
3. The rationality principle, a rule of conduct which dates back to before Socrates but which in relatively modern times was clarified in the writings of the eighteenth-century philosopher David Hume.
4. Arbitrage, which in finance theory is especially linked with the names of Professors Franco Modigliani and Merton Miller.

The insights of these people form the basic building blocks to understand modern portfolio choice and the attempt to come to grips with our overriding question as to the validity or not of portfolio indexing as an investment strategy. Do not be daunted by the grandiose names of these concepts—as we shall see, all the ideas can be readily understood with just a little thought.

SUBJECTIVE UTILITY

A starting point towards a theory of expectations is probability theory. This aims to quantify our expectations about the future in terms of a simple set of numbers ranging between zero (the impossible) to one (the inevitable). But what exactly are probabilities and how on earth do we measure them? Prior to Leonard Savage, there were various interpretations of probability, the dominant one being that probability is the relative frequency of an event with a set of trials, or the limit of the ratio of occurrences to trials within an infinite set of such trials. For example, if we say that when we throw a fair coin the 'probability' of a 'head' is one half or fifty per cent, what this means, according to the relative frequency approach, is that we might expect the number of 'heads' appearing, expressed as a ratio of the total number of trials, to be a number that comes closer and closer to one half as we increase the number of trials.

While such a view is one that many of us will be accustomed to from our school days, having had to throw a coin fifty times and to observe with each throw the ratio of heads to total throws, the approach has serious drawbacks. The most obvious one is that, in finance for example, many uncertain events that affect financial variables are not potentially repeatable under controlled experiment. This applies both to macro and micro events. Prior to Mexico entering the North American Free Trade Association (NAFTA), many observers wrote in terms of the 'high probability' of Mexico entering NAFTA. Currently (late 1998), many newspapers are carrying stories of the 'increasing possibility' of a global slowdown in 1999. Some doomsayers are predicting a 'high chance' of major technological failures in the global communications infrastructure at the turn of the millennium. Similarly you can read daily in the newspapers of the 'likelihood' of interest rate cuts or hikes by Central Banks in different countries. What do such phrases actually mean?

According to Savage, probabilities measure nothing else than degrees of belief. Probabilities of events are not 'objective' numbers that can be read off statistical tables for uncertain future events, but rather 'subjective' guesses about the likelihood of those events. On the surface this definition seems useful for finance theorists, as it neatly side-steps the problem of the non-repeatability of many events that affect financial variables. However, such a definition does not solve the question of how on earth we might measure in a consistent way these subjective probabilities. We may find a pessimist who confidently tells us that he believes the probability of a flood in his kitchen is ninety per cent and buys every house insurance policy he can find; there will be others who attach a much lower probability to such an event. More seriously for subjective utility theory, however, there may even be others who will hold their hands up in despair and tell us they simply do not know what the relevant probabilities are. On certain apparently reasonable assumptions about human behaviour, nonetheless, Savage showed that it was possible to elicit such probability information from a person by finding the odds at which that person would place a small wager on the event in question.

In simple terms the method to elicit these probabilities is as follows. Consider a fund manager called Rachael who states that she considers it 'likely' that shares will outperform bonds over the following twelve months, but thinks she cannot specify the likelihood in terms of probability. We then ask Rachael to play the following game.

We start out by offering her the choice between the following two options:

OPTION 1. If stocks do outperform bonds, she will get a bonus of $1000; otherwise she receives nothing.

OPTION 2. If a red ball is drawn at random from a bag containing $x\%$ red balls and $(1 - x)\%$ black balls, she will receive $1000. If a black ball is drawn, she receives nothing. We tell Rachael the particular value of x (for example we might start by saying the bag has 10% red balls and 90% black balls).

Assume Rachael says she prefers option 1 over option 2. We can then infer that Rachael considers it more likely that stocks will outperform bonds as greater than $x\%$. We then repeat the experiment for a slightly greater value of x and so on. Eventually through trial and error we should reach an x at which Rachael is indifferent between the two options. This x is then defined as the subjective probability that Rachael implicitly attaches to the likelihood that stocks will outperform bonds over the following year (for a fuller discussion of subjective utilities, see Box 1.2).

So the conclusion of Savage is that uncertainty about future events can be reduced to measurable subjective probabilities. This conclusion is an important plank in the overall framework of decision making under uncertainty to which we shall now turn.

Box 1.2 Can Rational Agents 'Agree to Disagree' Over the Odds?

At first glance, the Savage approach seems to leave open the possibility that 'anything goes' in terms of an individual's probability beliefs. If an individual says he believes with 99% probability that the plane he is due to travel on later that day will crash, it is perfectly rational to expect him to find an excuse not to fly. This notion has, unsurprisingly, troubled theorists, not to mention airlines!

An economist, Robert Aumann, has suggested a way out of the impasse. Return to the bond/stock problem in the main text. Suppose you attach a 75% probability to bonds outperforming stocks over a year, whereas I believe the correct probability to be just 25%. On this basis we should be able to enter into a small wager where I pay you an agreed amount, say $100, if bonds do outperform stocks and you will likewise pay me $100 if stocks outperform bonds. Fair enough?

Not so, according to Aumann! Notice that whereas the pay-off a year from now sums to zero (i.e. what I win you lose and vice-versa), this is not the case in terms of our expected pay-offs now—on entering the bet each of us believes we have an average or expected positive return of $50 (gaining $100 with probability 75% and only losing $100 with probability 25%—to get the average or expected return simply multiply each outcome by its probability). If we are both rational, we can only disagree because we have different information. By placing your bet on bonds over stocks you are effectively signalling to me that you have some information that I have not. Similarly, in my placing my bet on stocks over bonds, I am signalling that I have something up my sleeve that you do not know. Each of us should have our confidence shaken at the willingness of the other to bet against what we believe to be the proper odds. Consequently we shall wish to trade information, a process that should logically continue until we agree not to disagree over the true odds.

Aumann's conclusion—rational agents cannot agree to disagree over the probability of any defined future event. Do you agree? If not, why not? Try to think of circumstances where the Aumann result will not hold up. Thinking seriously about this will take you to the heart of what this book is about!

THE FORMALISATION OF UNCERTAINTY AS RISK

When I taught finance courses at university, I always used to read a health warning at this point—not only smoking can seriously damage your health; so too can thinking about uncertainty. Admittedly the material in this section is more difficult and challenging, but it is important to grasp the main points. Only then will the reader be properly equipped to understand the essence of some of the disputes in finance theory, including the issue of the relevance or otherwise of portfolio indexing. For those of you not trained in microeconomics, you may need to read this section twice. Try reading it quickly to grasp the main ideas and follow it with a more careful reading later.

The Role of Contingent Commodities

Kenneth Arrow was a powerful mathematician who developed several insights into various areas of decision making (see Box 1.3 for one of his interesting insights into democracy and its implications for fund management). In terms of our immediate purpose of analysing decision making under uncertainty, Arrow's ingenious achievement was to spell out clearly a set of circumstances where uncertainty would not hold out any fear for the investor who would be able to select his desired portfolio in the market place without difficulty, or if you like in terms of our earlier metaphor, he could pack his suitcase without fear for the weather. To understand this, we need to introduce the concept of a 'contingent' commodity. The first step in understanding what is meant by a contingent commodity is to realise that as well as having particular goods available for purchase and sale today (spot markets), individuals and companies also write contracts for deferred purchase and sale to some date in the future. These contracts are themselves then traded. A glance at any of the major financial newspapers will reveal that markets and trading in such so-called futures contracts does exist for many commodities ranging from crude oil to orange juice (see Table 1.2).

The second step is a simple expansion of the concept of a futures contract. Notice that in futures markets, the commodity is delivered at the pre-specified price come what may—the holder of the futures contract will receive his

Box 1.3 Asset Allocation by Committee—The Advantages of Tyranny Over Democracy

Kenneth Arrow's Nobel-prize-winning contribution came from examining another problem of decision making, that of decision making by a group of people. This also has implications for rational portfolio choice. Imagine a three-person, top-down asset allocation committee (Tom, Dick and Harry) is set up to decide a pension fund's allocation of funds between stocks, bonds and real estate. Depending on the ranking of the committee, the Chief Investment Officer (CIO) intends to put 50% of the portfolio in the first choice, 30% into the second choice, and 20% into the third choice. The CIO has chosen a committee of three so that there will be no problem—if there is disagreement, a majority vote will lead to a definite outcome. The committee duly meets and Tom, Dick and Harry give the following rankings based on their estimates of the likely returns for the three asset classes.

	TOM	DICK	HARRY
1st	Stocks	Bonds	Real Estate
2nd	Bonds	Real Estate	Stocks
3rd	Real Estate	Stocks	Bonds

The problem is the following. Note that there is a majority in favour of stocks over bonds (Tom and Harry); a majority in favour of bonds over real estate (Tom and Dick); and a majority in favour of real estate over stocks (Dick and Harry)! After much ado, the committee decides to retire to the bar and to appoint a sub-committee to examine how on earth this has happened. The CIO is not amused!

In fact our poor committee ought not to have been so surprised. In a famous theorem, Arrow proved that to guarantee consistent decisions in public choice and in other collective decision situations, it would be necessary to allow one person only to make decisions—long live tyranny!

Table 1.2 Futures Contracts

Orange Juice (CTN)—15 000 lbs; cents per lb

	Open	High	Low	Settle
Nov	117.90	118.00	115.50	115.55
Jan 99	120.15	120.40	118.00	118.10
Mar	122.00	122.00	120.10	120.10
May	123.00	123.40	121.60	122.00
July	123.70	124.00	123.50	123.50

Crude Oil, Light Sweet (NYM) 1000 bbls; $ per bbl

	Open	High	Low	Settle
Dec	14.24	14.45	13.86	14.42
Jan 99	14.41	14.63	14.08	14.80
Feb	14.54	14.82	14.30	14.80
Mar	14.71	14.98	14.48	14.96
Apr	14.72	15.15	14.72	15.12
May	14.97	15.02	14.88	15.27

Table shows market prices for quoted futures in orange juice and oil, with settlement deferred to different future dates.

Source: *The Wall Street Journal Europe*, Monday November 2, 1998 with permission.

barrel of oil or gallon of orange juice regardless of the state of the world at the agreed delivery date—come hell or high water the goods are delivered to the holder, unless of course he sells the contract to someone else who will then take delivery. Not only is it possible to write these futures contracts, it is also possible to write contingent futures contracts where goods will be purchased or sold at a future date only if certain pre-specified conditions are in place at the time of settlement of the contract. Again, such contracts are common in the financial world. Think of a holiday insurance contract, for example, where the insurance company agrees to bring the holder of the contract home, at zero cost to the holder, in an air ambulance only if the holder of the contract falls seriously ill while on holiday (but not if he does not fall seriously ill). Another form of contingent commodities contract which will be familiar to those working in financial markets is the options contract where the writer of the option guarantees to deliver the underlying asset (call option to the holder) or guarantees to buy it (put option to the holder) only in certain circumstances relating to the price of the underlying asset at some future date (see Table 1.3).

Table 1.3 Financial Options

Strike price $ tonne	—Calls—		—Puts—	
Aluminium (99.7%) *LME*	Nov	Feb	Nov	Feb
1250	75	106	1	16
1300	33	72	10	31
1350	9	46	35	54
Copper (Grade A) *LME*	Nov	Feb	Nov	Feb
1500	122	163	1	24
1600	40	98	19	58
1700	5	53	84	111
Coffee *LIFFE* (99.7%) *LME*	Nov	Jan	Nov	Jan
1600	100	73	1	45
1650	51	49	1	71
1700	12	32	12	104
Cocoa *LIFFE*	Dec	Mar	Dec	Mar
1000	32	65	10	16
1025	18	51	21	27
1050	10	40	38	41
Brent Crude *IPE*	Dec	Jan	Dec	Jan
1250	–	74	54	–
1300	29	52	–	94
1350	14	38	–	–

Table shows market prices of various commodity options, with different exercise prices and dates.

Source: *Financial Times*, Wednesday October 21, 1998. Reproduced by permission of the copyright holder.

To return to Arrow, in essence what he argued with regards to financial decision making under uncertainty was that if a full set of contingent futures markets existed for all goods and services, which were competitive and covered all future dates and all possible contingencies, then uncertainty need hold no fear for the investor. The investor could simply buy a set of contingent contracts to meet his needs in all eventualities.

To understand how Arrow reached this result, consider the following simple example. Although inherently conservative, Tom's recent move into the racy world of fund management straight from university has taken its toll on his lifestyle. Suppose Tom has $100 000 worth of assets, donated to him by a rich grandfather on obtaining his 'First' from Oxford. Like many budding male financial wizards, Tom has no time for his bank manager and too much time trying to show off to his two university sweethearts, an English rose and a Scottish maiden. That explains why Tom has $50 000 in a current account earning next to no interest and $50 000 invested in a flashy convertible (car, that is!). Suppose thc only uncertainty that Tom faces is the possibility of car theft and that this is extremely high in the area where he rents his flat. Specifically, according to the records of the insurance company, the chances of theft are a staggering 50%. Hence Tom faces two possible future states of the world: in the first no theft occurs and his wealth remains at $100 000; in the second his car gets stolen in which case not only will his rose and maiden desert him but he will be left with a mere $50 000, just enough for a new car but then he really is on the brink at the bank! Obviously as things stand Tom is faced with a potentially unpleasant degree of uncertainty given the high degree of crime in his area over which he has no control.

With this background, imagine Tom can trade in contingent commodities provided by a local insurance company. In particular, assume an insurance company offers competitive car-theft insurance contracts (the contingent commodity) at a 50% rate, i.e. \$100 of cover for \$50 of premium (we assume this because, if the insurance market is competitive, the insurance rate offered should be in line with the underlying odds). Armed with the ability to purchase these contracts, Tom can change his wealth distribution from either \$100 000 or \$50 000 to the range at which he feels most comfortable—see Figure 1.2). For example, if he fully insures, his wealth will be \$75 000 in either state of the world as can be verified from studying Figure 1.2.

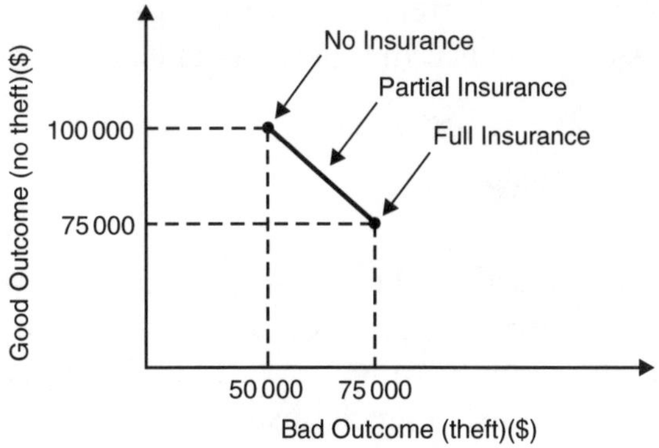

Figure 1.2 Changing Wealth Distribution Through Contingent Commodities

If Tom purchases *D* dollars of insurance and pays a premium of *D*/2 dollars (i.e. he pays the 50% rate), he changes his wealth distribution, depending on whether or not the car is actually stolen to the following:

IN THE EVENT THAT THE CAR IS STOLEN
\$50 000 (his cash) + *D* (his insurance claim) – *D*/2 (his premium)
IN THE EVENT THAT THE CAR IS NOT STOLEN
\$50 000 (his cash) + \$50 000 (value of his car) – *D*/2 (his premium)

Notice that in general, the slope of the feasible wealth pattern of Tom will be given by the formula $(-d/1-d)$ where d (small d) is the insurance rate (in our example 0.5 i.e. 50%). Why? By buying a total amount of insurance cover D, the individual gives up dD dollars in the 'good' state for $D-dD$ in the 'bad' state. Hence the slope of the line is given by the formula (check the graph where in our case the slope is simply -1 as can be checked by inserting 0.5 into the formula).

Thus the availability of insurance contracts has 'solved' Tom's potential quandary. More generally Arrow's world seems to solve the issue of uncertainty in one fell swoop. The need for divine revelation of the future is removed by the existence of competitively-priced contingent commodities. If a full set of contingent markets existed for all goods and services, individuals such as Tom would be spared the problems of decision making under uncertainty not just about their motor cars but about uncertainty related to any good or service; they could simply trade contingent commodities to reach their desired wealth patterns over time regardless of the particular states of the world that actually emerge.

The Role of Expected Utility

So far Arrow's analysis has alerted us to the possibility that if a full set of contingent markets existed, this would potentially allow us as individuals to cope with uncertainty through simple use of the market mechanism. However, one issue which Arrow's analysis leaves open is what particular bunch of contingent commodities an individual will choose. Putting this in terms of our simple car-theft insurance problem, we have as yet no idea about Tom's preferences when faced with uncertainty and how this will affect how much insurance he will actually buy. Will he fully insure? Will he partially insure? Maybe he will not insure at all. Is there a way to find out what is optimal for Tom?

Enter John Von Neumann, another outstanding mathematician generally remembered for his work on the modern computer and more controversially for his contributions to the Manhattan project for the development of atomic weaponry during the Second World War despite his ailing health and confinement to a wheelchair (film buffs—ever seen Dr Strangelove? Who do you think the role model for Strangelove was?). Working together with his colleague Oskar Morgenstern, what Von Neumann did was to suggest that it is possible to define preferences over all these contingent commodities using a cardinal scale (a scale like we use for height or temperature), and moreover that there is a simple rule to calculate the overall preferences an individual will have between various actions which entail uncertain consequences, using this cardinal scale. This rule is called the expected utility rule (and in Box 1.4 you will see that interest in the expected utility rule has been around for a long time in some of the strangest places!).

Box 1.4 The St. Petersburg Paradox

History shows that attempts to come to grips with decision making under uncertainty have their roots in the analysis of betting games. An excellent introduction to the history and the development of the various concepts is Peter Bernstein's *Against the Gods*. Ironically, gambling seems to have been of particular interest to the ecclesiastical profession! Anyway, by the eighteenth century, Daniel Bernouilli was already well on the way to formalising an expected-utility model of decision making under uncertainty.

Bernouilli started his analysis with a simple betting game, usually referred to as the St. Petersburg paradox. The story goes like this. For a price, Peter offers Paul the chance to play the following game. A coin is tossed and if it falls 'heads', Peter pays Paul \$2; if it falls tails, the coin is retossed, and this time if it falls 'heads', Peter pays Paul \$4; if however it falls tails again the coin is retossed and this time Peter will pay Paul \$8 if it falls 'heads', if not the coin will be tossed again with the 'payoff for the 'head' again doubled. The game continues until a head appears. The question is how much should Paul be prepared to pay Peter to play the game.

In terms of expected values, the answer is apparently an infinite sum, as the expected value of the above game is infinite. To see this, remember that the expected value of any uncertain income stream of this type is simply defined as the sum of the probability of each outcome multiplied by the payoff in each outcome. A 'head' on the first toss of a fair coin has probability $\frac{1}{2}$; the probability of a head first appearing on the second toss is $\frac{1}{4}$ etc. Hence the expected value of the game can be written:

$$\text{Expected Value} = \tfrac{1}{2}(\$2) + \tfrac{1}{4}(\$4) + \tfrac{1}{8}(\$8) \text{ etc. } \textit{ad infinitum}$$

$$= 1 + 1 + 1 \text{ etc. } \textit{ad infinitum}$$

The above sum has no finite limit. But obviously no one in their right mind would pay an infinite amount to play the game—and hence the paradox. Bernouilli's resolution was to suggest that, as a person's wealth increases, additional units of income become progressively less valuable. In other words, a person's 'utility' rises at a declining rate with increases in income. This implies the prospect of a certain sum x will be preferred to a gamble having the same expected value x (if you are not sure why, read Box 1.5). This is usually referred to as risk aversion. In simple terms a risk averse person prefers \$1 for certain to a 50: 50 chance of either \$2 or nothing, because \$2 has less utility than twice the utility of \$1. Conversely, a risk lover will prefer the gamble to the certain outcome.

If Paul is risk averse, Bernouilli argued, it is quite conceivable that he will only pay a modest amount to play the game. The paradox has apparently been resolved.

Perhaps the best way to get an understanding of cardinal scales and the expected utility rule is to move briefly away from the dizzy heights of finance theory and onto the golf course! Imagine you are about to leave the clubhouse to play a game of golf with an old friend. If possible, you would like to walk around the course to work off a few kilos. Unfortunately, the starter informs you that the local meteorological office says that there is a 50% chance of rain. Do you forget the walk and hire a buggy instead to protect you if the heavens open? The answer depends on your strength of preference between walking in the dry, walking in the wet, driving in the dry and driving in the wet. If, for example, you are a true Scot and relish walking in the dry a good deal more than you fear getting drenched, then you may well risk it. If however you are a little wimpish (no nations mentioned!) you may prefer the buggy. To decide, we need information on your strength of preference.

A cardinal preference scale does just that. Assume for the minute we have a way to calculate it (see Box 1.5 if you are interested in how to do this). Assume that the four possibilities above have associated pleasure rankings of 10 (walking in the dry), 0 (walking in the rain), 3 (driving in the dry) and 5 (driving in the rain). Then the average or expected utility of walking is 5 (50% of 10 plus 50% of 0) and the average or expected utility of driving is only 4 (50% of 3 plus 50% of 5). Such a person will walk on the expected utility rule. But imagine the pay-offs had been 8, 0, 6, and 4. Then the expected utility of walking would only have been 4, but that of driving 5. According to the expected utility rule, a person with these preferences will hire the buggy and forget the kilos!

Box 1.5 Constructing Cardinal Utility Scales

The distinguishing feature of a cardinal scale is that while various possible scales are imaginable to measure the same thing, which differ either in zero point or in unit interval (temperature measured in Fahrenheit or Centigrade; height measured in feet or metres), relative magnitudes remain unchanged (e.g. approximately speaking doubling three feet three inches is the same as doubling one metre).

Now imagine that we think about a person faced with uncertain consequences but where these consequences are summarised by the amount of income he will have. Specifically in a worst case, he will be left broke ($0); in the bliss case he will have a windfall of $100 000. Now consider a level of income lying between $0 and $100 000, say $25 000. Imagine the individual is faced with a choice of $25 000 for certain and a 'reference lottery' offering $100 000 with an assigned

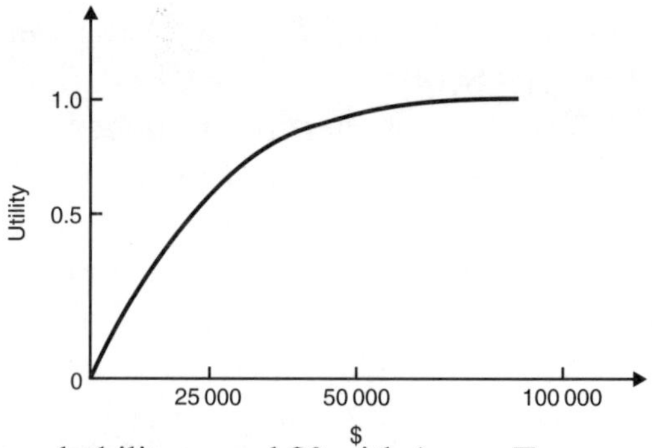

probability p, and \$0 with $1 - p$. For a very high p, say 0.99, most individuals will prefer the gamble (big chance of a windfall of \$100 000 versus the certainty of \$25 000). For a very small p, however, most individuals will prefer the certainty of \$25 000. At some value of p, the individual will be indifferent between the gamble and the certain outcome. We mark this p on the vertical axis as the cardinal utility associated with \$25 000. For the sake of simplicity, let us assume this point is 0.5. Repeating the experiment for all income levels allows us to draw out a cardinal scale between 0 and 1, which represent a cardinal measure of utility for any consequence so long as we confine measuring consequences by the amount of income received in that state.

Using such a graph, you can now formalise Bernoulli's resolution to the St. Petersburg paradox. Any individual that has a 'concave' graph for cardinal utility will prefer the certainty of a given income to the 50: 50 chance of that same income (see below). For example, \$25 000 for certain yields more than the average utility of the 50: 50 chance of either \$50 000 or \$0, which only yields expected utility of $\frac{1}{2}(0) + \frac{1}{2}(< 1) = \; < 0.5$.

Now the important point of the golf course example is that cardinal utilities defined on each possible outcome, together with the expected utility rule, potentially provide a route for deciding optimal actions to take when confronted with uncertainty. For those of you who want to follow this logic through for the case of Tom and the car-theft example, refer to Box 1.6.

Box 1.6 Using the Expected Utility Rule to Identify Optimal Decisions—The Case of Tom again

Using the analysis of Box 5, the first thing we need to do is to transform the consequence matrix facing Tom in terms of income, to a consequence matrix in terms of utility. Assume Tom's utility function is concave and can be represented by the precise formula $f(c) = \sqrt{(c/100\,000)}$. That will give us the consequence matrix and associated utilities below.

Consequence Matrix Facing Tom

Actions	***States***	
	Car stolen (prob 50%)	Not stolen (prob 50%)
Do not insure	\$50 000	\$100 000
Partially insure	\$50 000–\$75 000	\$100 000–\$75 000
Fully insure	\$75 000	\$75 000

Cardinal Measure of Tom's Preferences

Actions	***States***	
	Car stolen (prob 50%)	Not stolen (prob 50%)
Do not insure	0.707	1.000
Partially insure	0.707–0.866	1.000–0.866
Fully insure	0.866	0.866

Then to attach a utility number to any action that Tom might make, we simply multiply the various consequences possible for each action by the associated utility. For example, to calculate the utility associated with the action 'do not insure', we have:

$$U\text{ (no insurance)} = 0.5\,(0.707) + 0.5\,(1.000) = 0.853$$

Again for the action 'fully insure' we have:

$$U\text{ (full insurance)} = 0.5\,(0.866) + 0.5\,(0.866) = 0.866$$

Hence in our example, Tom will prefer to fully insure than not to insure. In fact you might like to satisfy yourself that this preference for full insurance will also hold over partial insurance (try it for a specific example). In fact it is possible to prove that a risk-averse individual will always fully insure, if offered competitive insurance rates. As a prelude to Chapter 3, can you think of any reason why an insurance company might not, however, be prepared to offer, fully competitive insurance rates. Hint: if Tom fully insures at the competitive rate, what incentive does he have to look after his car properly?

Imagine Tom now has a friend 'Mad Max' who is money crazy, a real product of Dostoyevsky's *The Gambler*, and whose cardinal utility function is convex (gets steeper as wealth rises). In this case, Max will not insure at all, as increased risk gives increased pleasure. Max prefers to run the risk of having his car stolen rather than giving a dime to the poor insurance salesman. Try to construct a convex function to prove this result using the above analysis as a guide.

It is time to summarise a little. What we have been doing is creating a framework to help us to identify optimal actions when confronted with uncertainty. If we can rely on the existence of meaningful probabilities, the existence of a full set of contingent commodities, and the ability to rank these contingent commodities in a consistent way using cardinal utilities and the expected utility rule, we now potentially have a means to do just that. We seem to have come a long way from the apparent despair of the first section!

THE RATIONALITY PRINCIPLE

The rationality principle as the term is used in finance embraces two concepts. The first is that the decision maker is able to set out all of his feasible alternatives and then to rank these alternatives consistently along the lines of the previous section; the second is that the decision maker will actually choose that alternative which maximises his preferences. Someone who does this is referred to as being 'instrumentally rational', a tradition in philosophy which in relatively modern times is attributed to David Hume and his famous 'Treatise on Human Nature'. Reason is, in Hume's view, 'the slave of the passions and can never pretend to any other office than to serve and to obey them' a far cry from the view of the Greeks that it was our ability to reason that set us apart from the animals. The instrumentally rational person has preferences—fish over meat, classical over rock music, brunettes over blondes—and is deemed rational by choosing actions that best satisfy those preferences.

To some extent the assumption of instrumental rationality may seem reasonable at first sight—after all it would seem somewhat absurd for someone to deliberately choose an action knowing that a better one was available. For the moment we shall leave it at that, but readers should beware that, when the world is blurred, it may not be so easy to rank alternatives easily. And even if we can rank alternatives, we shall see that there are still a few paradoxes that are hard to unravel. Further, we shall see that the parametric approach to rationality assumed in finance (with the investor taking his environment as constant and as something over which he now has control) is something which skips over much of what is important in financial markets, including the important concept of strategic decision making. Strategic rationality can be particularly difficult to define. In short, defining what is the rational thing to do in complex financial markets may not be anywhere near as straightforward as simple examples of instrumental rationality might suggest.

ARBITRAGE

The final pillar of modern portfolio theory is arbitrage, a concept that in finance most people first come across when examining the theory of a company's optimal capital structure first developed by Franco Modigliani and Merton Miller (MM henceforth). Arbitrage is a process whereby specialist traders iron out price discrepancies between goods of the same type. MM argued that, under certain circumstances, a company's debt/equity ratio should have no bearing on its overall value in capital markets, challenging intuition which might suggest that a high degree of gearing (that is a high ratio of debt to equity in a company's balance sheet) might lower the value of the firm because of the increased risk of default on debt-interest payments. Their underlying idea can be understood in simple terms by considering a firm's balance sheet. On the 'left' side we have the company's real assets such as plant and machinery. On the 'right' side we have the paper liabilities used to fund these assets. The idea that one can create true value by shuffling the mix of paper liabilities seems unlikely. MM proved the suspicion of alchemy with a simple arbitrage argument.

The reasoning goes as follows. Imagine for the moment that two identical companies in terms of operating assets and market environment had different enterprise values (where enterprise value is defined as the sum of the market value of the debt and equity instruments issued by the company to fund its real assets). In a world where arbitrage is possible, a moment's thought will confirm that such a state cannot persist for long. Why not? Abstracting from government and taxes, there are only two claims on a company's operating earnings—the fixed claim of debt holders and the residual claim of shareholders. To ensure full entitlement to a firm's operating earnings, one could simply buy the outstanding debt and equity of that company. But if the sum of the two firms' debt and equity values were different, while the operating earnings from those two companies were the same, obviously no one would buy the more expensive debt/equity package. The arbitrageur would buy the less expensive package and sell the more expensive package and in so doing iron out the discrepancy in valuation.

CONCLUSIONS

The various concepts discussed in this chapter—subjective probabilities, the framework for analysing uncertainty as risk, the rationality principle and arbitrage are the cornerstones for the development of the modern theory of finance. In particular they underlie a model of capital market behaviour which we shall meet in the next chapter, which suggests that passive portfolio indexing is the optimal action for the investor. It is to this model, and to the growth of indexing in practice in financial markets, that we now turn.

2

The Capital Asset Pricing Model—The Dawn of Portfolio Indexing

INTRODUCTION

The view that the best way for any individual to manage a portfolio is simply to invest in all available assets in proportion to their market capitalisation has its roots in the Capital Asset Pricing Model (CAPM). As we shall see, CAPM has devastating conclusions for both stock pickers and asset allocators alike. In brief, CAPM suggests that portfolio indexing is the only logical strategy for investors—stock picking is irrelevant and asset allocation is simplicity itself as all investors need to do is to invest in the market index. How are these striking conclusions reached?

Let us go back to Tom. Having now fully insured himself against the possibility of losing his car, which cost him a massive \$25 000 premium, his private-client stockbroker Jonathan has now called him with a new proposal on a way to invest his \$25 000 cash left after he has paid his insurance bill. Jonathan's idea is for Tom to buy an equity index fund as a first step into the 'real' world of finance—the world of stock markets! However, Tom is not stupid. Remembering Woody Allen's definition of a stockbroker as someone who advises his friends on how to invest their wealth until all that wealth has disappeared, Tom wants some clear guidance on the best investment advice for someone in his position. He certainly does not want to lose everything he has left! Hence the book on Portfolio Theory is opened!

PORTFOLIO THEORY

The father of modern finance, Harry Markowitz, was one of the first people to draw together the various concepts of Chapter 1 to produce a model designed to select optimal portfolios for investors. Amazingly he did it almost by accident when he was a mere twenty five years old, as a by-product of his main interest in those days, linear programming. The steps in his thinking were as follows:

1. Using the concept of probability (Savage), and the analysis of uncertainty as risk (Arrow), Markowitz showed how it was possible to identify a set of efficient portfolios from which any individual could choose his desired risk/return package (in much the same way that it was possible to identify a set of possible insurance levels for Tom in Chapter 1, from zero insurance to full insurance).
2. Using the concept of utility (Von Neumann), and the rationality principle (Hume), he then showed how any individual could and would select a unique optimal portfolio to suit his own preferences concerning risk (in much the same way that Tom and Max could use the insurance market in Chapter 1 to choose their desired levels of insurance which we can recall from Chapter 1 Box 1.6 was for Tom to fully insure and for Max not to insure at all).

The first step can best be understood by simply considering two company shares in which an investor might invest. The results we shall derive can easily be extended to any number of shares, but may require the use of a computer! Imagine our two shares are drawn from very different industries, say the international oil exploration and domestic construction industries. For simplicity, assume the industries are completely 'independent', with each industry having a 50:50 chance of good times or bad. As the industries are independent, the good times for the oil stock, say a major exploration discovery, will have no influence on whether or not our construction company's share will have a good year or not, which we can assume will instead depend on the fortunes of the domestic economy. Notice that the important word here is 'influence'—it is not that we will never observe good times in both industries, rather that when such an occurrence emerges, it is driven by chance. In other words, we are not considering a situation as between, say, the automobile production sector and car components sector, where it seems reasonable to assume non-independence, that is the fortunes of the car production sector will almost inevitably have a direct influence on the car components sector.

We can draw out a consequence matrix of possible outcomes for the oil stock/construction stock example (Table 2.1), using the building blocks of the last chapter. In the good state, the oil stock will give a 20% return but if there is no oil discovery, returns will be zero. The construction stock has a similar pattern of returns; if the economy is strong, returns will be 20%, but if the economy is weak, the construction stock will likewise give zero returns.

From Table 2.1 we can also calculate the various returns that will emerge if an investor puts 50% of his money into the oil stock and 50% into the construction stock. Remember that the good/bad states in each industry are independent—that means that while there is a 50:50 chance of the oil share doing well, in only half the times that this happens

Table 2.1 Returns from the Oil and Construction Stocks Undiversified and Diversified

Undiversified Returns

Oil Stock Returns (%)

Discovery	No Discovery	Expected Return
20%	0%	10%

Construction Stock Returns (%)

Strong Econ.	Weak Econ.	Expected Return
20%	0%	10%

Diversified (50% in each share)

		Oil Stock	
		Good State	Bad State
Construction Stock	Good State	20%	10%
	Bad State	10%	0%

To understand the matrix of diversified returns, consider for example what happens in the GOOD/BAD world (good for the oil stock, bad for the construction stock). On that half of your money invested in the oil stock you will earn a 20% return. On the half invested in the construction stock you will earn a 0% return. That will give you an average return of 10% (that is $\frac{1}{2}(20\%) + \frac{1}{2}(0\%)$. The same reasoning can be used to calculate all entries in the matrix. Notice that any entry in this matrix has a 25% probability—for example to calculate the chances of seeing both an oil discovery and strong domestic economy we multiply together their individual probabilities $(50\%) \times (50\%) = 25\%$. In words, on only half the occasions where we observe an oil discovery will the domestic economy be strong at the same time. Notice also that the expected return on the diversified portfolio is 10% (multiply each outcome by its respective probability to see this), but that the risks of 0% in the diversified portfolio case are half those versus the undiversified case (25% versus 50%).

will the construction share also do well. Similarly, when the construction company is doing well on the back of a strong domestic economy, on only half of those occasions will an oil find lead to similar good fortune at the oil exploration company. Hence in the lower part of Table 2.1 each consequence has a 25% probability (e.g. there is a 25% chance of both the oil company and the construction company doing well etc.).

And now the crux. Through diversification (that is owning both shares), an investor can change the nature of the risks that he faces. Whereas if he only owned the oil share his maximum upside was 20% but he risked a 0% return with 50% probability, giving an average or expected return of 10%, with a diversified portfolio consisting of half of his money in each share, he still has an expected return of 10% but his chance of a 0% return has been cut to 25%. This is the benefit that diversification potentially brings.

Finance theorists conventionally measure of diversification in terms of a statistic called the standard deviation or 'volatility' of the portfolio. Just to make things look difficult, this statistic is usually written as the Greek symbol σ. The standard deviation of the portfolio in turn obviously depends on the standard deviation of the individual shares comprising the portfolio and, crucially on the interaction of these standard deviations between the different shares in the portfolio. This interaction is usually measured by another statistic derived from the standard deviations of the individual shares and is referred to as the correlation coefficient between the shares. Thankfully, this statistic at least is normally written with the roman lettering r! Anyway, all this, and the rather daunting formulas used to calculate standard deviations and correlation coefficients are discussed further in Box 2.1.

Box 2.1 Standard Deviations and Correlation Coefficients

The standard deviation of return attempts to measure the dispersion of the possible outcomes making up the expected return. How can we formalise this notion? Let us go back to the parameters of the oil stock/construction stock example. To calculate the implied standard deviation of each stock, we first calculate the expected return on each stock; then we calculate the variance of each stock defined as the sum of the deviation from the mean of each outcome squared, multiplied by the relevant probability; finally we take the square root of this number to obtain the standard deviation. In figures:

Standard Deviation of either Oil Share or Construction Share

(Outcome–Mean)	*(Outcome–Mean)*^{2} = *V*	*PR (Outcome)* × *V*
20%–10% = 10%	0.01	0.5 (0.01) = 0.005
0%–10% = – 10%	0.01	0.5 (0.01) = 0.005
Sum		0.01

Square Root = Standard Deviation Share = 10.0%

What about the standard deviation of a portfolio comprising 50% of the portfolio in each of the two shares? From the numbers in the text we have:

Standard Deviation of 50:50 Portfolio

(Outcome–Mean)	*(Outcome–Mean)*^{2} = *V*	*PR (Outcome)* × *V*
20%–10% = 10%	0.01	0.25(0.01) = 0.0025
10%–10% = 0%	0	0.25(0) = 0
10%–10% = 0%	0	0.25(0) = 0
0%–10% = – 10%	0.01	0.25(0.01) = 0.0025
Sum		0.005

Square Root = Standard Deviation of Portfolio = 7.1%

The crucial point here is that the portfolio standard deviation cannot be calculated as simply as we calculated the expected return on the portfolio, that is, the portfolio standard deviation is not simply the probability weighted average of the standard deviation of the individual shares (which would be 10%, that is 0.5(10%) + 0.5(10%) = 10%) but is substantially less. That is the advantage of diversification. More generally, portfolio variance (in the two share case labelling the shares A and B) can be written as:

$$\text{Variance (Portfolio)} = w^2\sigma_A{}^2 + (1-w)^2\sigma_B{}^2 + 2w(1-w)\sum_{i=1}^{n}(a_i - \mathrm{E(A)})(b_i - \mathrm{E(B)})pr(i).$$

where w is the weight of the portfolio in asset A, standard deviations are marked with a σ, E(A) is the expected value of A, and a_i for example is the return of A in the ith state of the world and $pr(i)$ is the associated probability.

The square root of this horrible looking term gives us portfolio volatility. As you can see, this expression is not the weighted average of the variances of A and B as was the case for expected return. The final component of the expression is a difficult-looking term which describes the relationship between the returns on A and B. This term (excluding the terms in *w*) is called the covariance of returns between A and B. Sometimes finance texts prefer to standardise covariances by putting them on a scale from $-1-$ to $+1$. This can be achieved by dividing the covariance by the product of the standard deviations of the shares, and the resulting number is referred to as the correlation coefficient between A and B. When shares are perfectly correlated the correlation coefficient is $+1$; when they are perfectly negatively correlated it is -1, etc. Any major statistics book will show how to derive the correlation coefficient from covariances.

Extension to a multi-share case is straightforward mathematically but tedious. Again any major statistic book will derive the results for those interested. In practice, a computer program can be used to calculate multi-share covariances or correlation coefficients.

You may be relieved to know that we can skip merrily over Box 2.1, at least at a first reading, and concentrate on some general principles. The interesting question is to analyse what determines the extent of the potential benefits that an investor can hope to enjoy through diversification. Unsurprisingly the crucial factor is the degree to which the fortunes of the various companies (in our simple case just two companies) are, or are not, linked. There are actually three interesting cases to analyse; the case where the two shares fortunes are perfectly linked together in each state of the world (perfectly correlated securities); the case where the two shares react in exactly opposite ways in each state of the world (perfectly negatively correlated securities); and the final (most likely) case where the fortunes of the two companies are linked, but less than perfectly.

Figure 2.1 summarises the benefits of diversification in

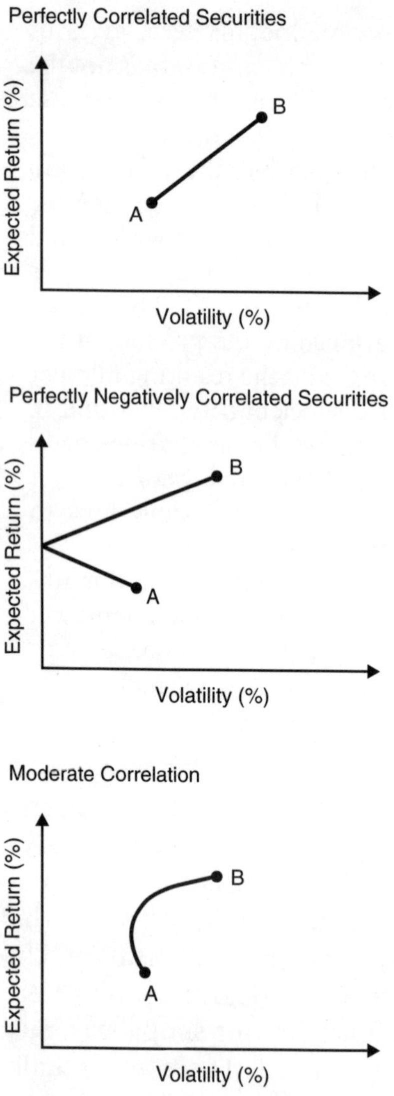

Figure 2.1 The Benefits of Diversification

Notice that when shares are perfectly negatively correlated, it is possible to construct a portfolio of the two shares with no risk. We shall come across this result later in the Chapter each of these cases. In each example, the line drawn on the graph is referred to as the efficiency frontier which shows what happens to overall portfolio returns and risks for different combinations of the two shares. And although we have drawn up these efficiency frontiers for a hypothical two-stock world, a moment's thought will reveal that, since we can describe all portfolios, regardless of the number of stocks, simply in terms of portfolio expected return and portfolio standard deviation and then mark the portfolio on our 'map', we can draw up an efficiency frontier for any number of stocks or portfolios we care to mention. Indeed in the limit we can construct these efficiency frontiers for stocks and portfolios from countries drawn from all over the world. Patrick Odier (of private Swiss bank Lombard Odier fame) has studied such efficiency frontiers, and an example of the type of benefits one can typically gain from international diversification and from diversification into bonds as well as stocks can be seen in Figure 2.2.

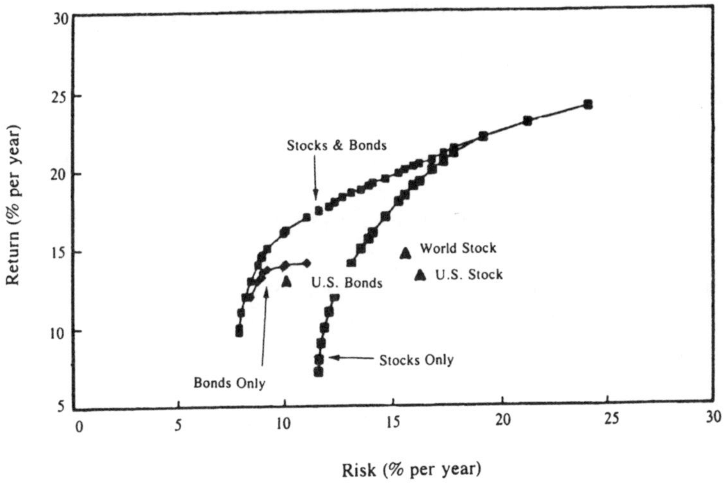

Figure 2.2 An International Efficiency Frontier

Source: Odier, P. and Solnik, B. 1993. Lessons for international asset allocation. *Financial Analysts Journal*, 49, 63–77.

So far we have seen how the concepts of probability and consequences can be used to define an efficiency frontier. All we need now do is to define a cardinal utility function over all possible combinations of risk and return. Canny readers will be aware that this is a slight simplification on the Von Neumann utility function of Chapter 1, and those interested in the exact relationship can follow up the story in Box 2.2. The really important point to understand is that if an investor is risk averse, we might expect his utility function to have the shape as in Figure 2.3. Why? Think of each of the lines as a contour on a map, but replace 'height' by 'utility'—just as on a conventional map the contour traces out the spots on the map at the same height, so our utility contour traces out combinations of risk and return giving the investor the same level of utility. The curved shape of each contour simply reflects that as the investor takes on additional units of risk, the return required becomes ever greater if he is to remain at

Box 2.2 Mean Standard Deviation Utility and Von Neumann Utility

In many situations, mean/standard deviation utility acts as a simplification of the Von Neumann expected utility rule and will give the same ranking of uncertain prospects. That is handy as it potentially saves us the trouble of having to do complex calculations over all possible states of the world—instead we simply summarise an uncertain prospect by its mean and standard deviation. However, unfortunately the two approaches do not always rank prospects the same way.

Imagine a share A that has a 90% chance of giving a return of 4% but a 10% chance of yielding 14%. Also imagine another share B that has a 90% chance of giving a 6% return but which also has a 10% chance of losing you money, specifically a −4% return. The steps involved in calculating the standard deviation of each share are summarised below. First we calculate the average or mean return of each share, and the standard deviation of each share:

Mean Return of A	Mean Return of B
0.9 (4%) + 0.1 (14%) = 5%	0.9 (6%) + 0.1 (− 4%) = 5%

Standard Deviation of A

(Outcome–Mean)	*(Outcome–Mean)*^{2} = *V*	PR *(Outcome)* × *V*
− 1%	0.0001	0.9 (0.0001) = 0.00009
9%	0.0081	0.1 (0.0081) = 0.00081
Sum		0.0009

Square Root = Standard Deviation of A = 3.0%

Standard Deviation of B

(Outcome–Mean)	*(Outcome–Mean)* = *V*	*PR (Outcome)* × *V*
1%	0.0001	0.9 (0.0001) = 0.00009
− 9%	0.0081	0.1 (0.0081) = 0.00081
Sum		0.0009

Square Root = Standard Deviation of B = 3.0%

So both shares have a 5% expected return and both have a standard deviation of return of 3%. Under a mean variance utility ranking, an investor should be indifferent between the two shares. But would you be indifferent between A and B? Many people would prefer A on the grounds that B involves the possibility of a monetary loss. As an exercise for those of you that are mathematically minded, check that a Von Neumann utility function calculated on each of the consequences, together with the expected utility rule will lead to a 'correct' ordering of A and B. You can use a cubic-root function for example to deal with the problem that the square root of a negative number is not a defined real number.

For us the important point to grasp is that the mean–standard deviation rule may at times lead to deceptive orderings of prospects. Nevertheless, it is generally used in finance if only because of the considerable ease it brings to calculation when faced with complex prospects—all we need estimate are the mean and standard deviation of any such prospect which most modern calculators can easily compute.

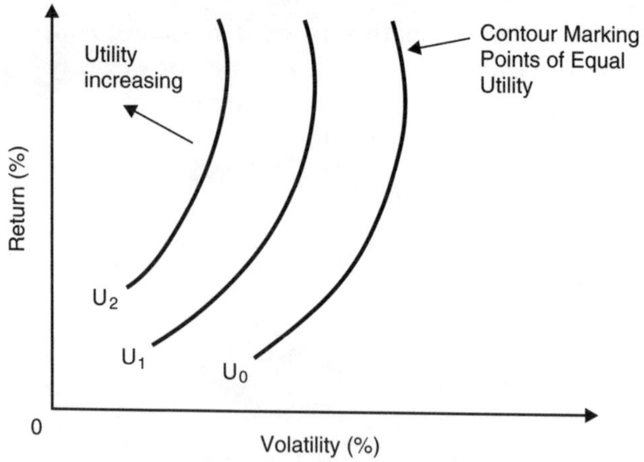

Figure 2.3 The Utility Function of a Risk Averse Investor

the same utility. Remember we are assuming our investor is risk averse. As we move towards the north west of the graph, the utility mountain becomes ever higher, reflecting the fact that 'return' is a 'good thing' while risk is a 'bad thing'. The method we can use to construct such a utility map has already been outlined in Chapter 1.

The fundamental result of portfolio theory can now be seen clearly by combining the efficiency frontier with the utility map. Stating the result succinctly, we can say that each investor will place himself on the efficiency frontier at that point where the rate at which he is prepared to substitute risk and return (the slope of his utility contour) is equal to the rate at which he can substitute risk and return in the market place as delineated by the efficiency frontier. For two different individuals, we have drawn the optimal portfolios (Figure 2.4). The actual portfolio chosen by any individual depends crucially on the shape of his utility function, and hence on his attitude towards risk.

Notice an important implication of this result. In the world of portfolio theory, investors may well hold different portfolios and there can be no presumption that holding a market index is optimal for all investors. Depending on

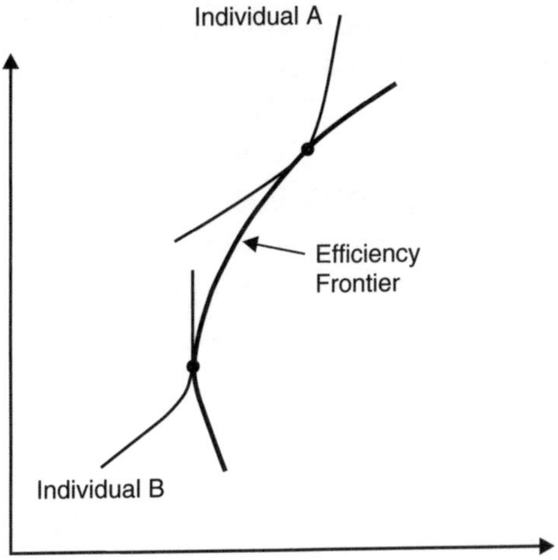

Figure 2.4 Optimal Portfolios for Different Individuals

Both individuals are risk averse but relatively, speaking, A is prepared to take on more risk than B compensated for by a greater expected return

their attitudes towards risk, some individuals will prefer riskier portfolios weighted towards riskier assets such as shares in oil exploration companies; others will prefer 'safer' portfolios weighted towards sectors such as electrical utilities and other 'bond-type' investments including not just bonds themselves but other low volatility equities such as motorway and water concessions etc. The crucial variable is each individual's preferences towards risk—the portfolio theory of Markowitz *per se* does not at all recommend indexing as the best strategy available to investors.

A further point to note is that while we have drawn up the efficiency frontier as identical for our two individuals in Figure 2.4, there is no need in portfolio theory for each individual's efficiency frontier to be the same. If two individuals have different expectations concerning the potential risks and returns of various investments, they will obviously then have different efficiency frontiers. In other words, in the world of portfolio theory, we are prepared to admit the case that individuals might have different expectations regarding future returns and volatility of different stocks and this will evidently affect the securities they will decide to hold. Even if two different individuals have identical attitudes to risk, if their perceptions of future risks and returns on securities differ, then they will hold different portfolios.

Indeed not only does portfolio theory concede that different investors might decide to hold different portfolios of stocks, it also suggests that individuals may well choose relatively concentrated portfolios consisting of a strictly limited number of stocks. In practice, an investor can choose between a vast array of shares. The question is how quickly does overall portfolio risk decrease as we increase the potential for diversification? Figure 2.5 draws out a typical relationship between portfolio risk and the number of shares held. Typically a portfolio of just ten shares exhausts about ninety per cent of the possible gains of diversification. Even just a few assets, carefully chosen, can cut total portfolio risk substantially, especially when these assets have substantially different risk characteristics. Again,

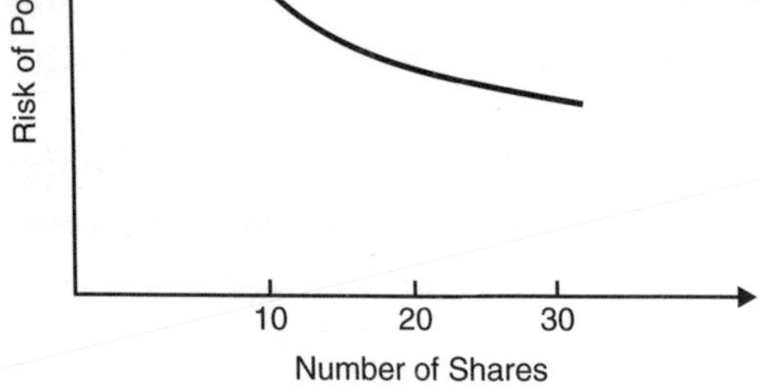

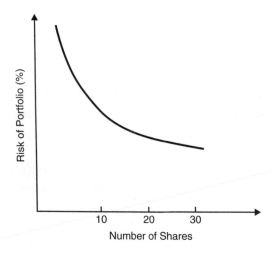

Figure 2.5 The Benefits of More Shares in a Portfolio

Even with just ten carefully chosen securities, portfolio risk can be substantially reduced

this is a far cry from passive portfolio indexing where the investor may actually be exposed to the movements of a substantial number of shares depending on the index—for example the FT All Share Index that we first met in the introduction to this book comprises over 850 shares!

THE CAPM TWIST

At this point you might be justified in wondering if anyone would ever invest in an index fund, given the analysis to date. Tom certainly was, and the idea of investing his last \$25 000 in Jonathan's index fund did not at all seem like a good idea. Surely each individual should choose his portfolio based on his own attitude towards risk? However, Tom noticed that there was another section to the portfolio analysis book that he thought he had better read before ringing Jonathan back. This was a section on CAPM. Reading on, what Tom realised was that the developer of CAPM, Professor William Sharpe, made several major additional assumptions to the analysis above but, as we shall see, the price for these additional assumptions seemed worth paying as they led to simpler and more dramatic results than the Markowitz analysis. These additional assumptions were:

1. As well as being able to invest in a set of risky equities, an investor could also invest in a riskless government bond (riskless in the sense of having a guaranteed return with no variability attached to that return). Not only can individuals invest in this riskless asset, but they can also borrow unlimited amounts of funds at this same riskless rate.
2. Individual investors are assumed to be fully informed, and able to describe the risks and returns on all securities in terms of expected return and standard deviation, along the lines of Markowitz. However, they are now also assumed to have identical

expectations about the risks and returns of these different securities, unlike the case of portfolio theory (in terms of the discussion in Chapter 1, we do not allow individuals to agree to disagree—see Box 1.2 from Chapter 1 on Aumann).

3. Sharpe also assumes that all investors have identical investment horizons, and hence we abstract from issues that might arise if some investors 'trade' over the short term while others 'lock in' for longer-term returns.
4. Finally we assume a frictionless market where arbitrage (Modigliani and Miller) immediately irons out possible price discrepancies between securities. Frictionless markets technically rule out other distorting factors such as transactions costs and taxes which can prevent perfect arbitrage.

This is probably quite a lot to swallow, I can almost hear you saying. However, all models are to some degree simplifications of underlying reality and what is important is whether the additional cost of these assumptions is potentially worth it in terms of new discoveries and the predictions of the regenerated model. In the case of CAPM, there is at least a case for reading further, as with the additional assumptions come simpler and more radical conclusions than in portfolio theory.

Sharpe showed that these assumptions radically changed the shape of the efficiency frontier facing every individual. In particular, the efficiency frontier will now be linear and identical for all individuals. The slope of this CAPM efficiency frontier is crucial in finance and is referred to as the price of risk (Figure 2.6). Notice that the slope of this line happens to be the expected return on one particular portfolio labelled M on the original efficiency frontier minus the yield on the riskless security, all divided by the standard deviation of the particular portfolio M.

What is this portfolio M? Rather than wading through a

lot of uncomfortable mathematics which could also lead us to the answer, we can proceed by stating what it is and then by considering why this must be right! M is the portfolio of all risky assets weighted by their respective market capitalisations. The reason why is because all securities that are in the market must be held by someone. Imagine a security was overpriced and no buyer could be found. Then since we have arbitrage in CAPM, an arbitrageur would sell this security short, driving its price down (and hence its expected future return up) until the price found an equilibrium where the stock was willingly held. Using this logic we can see that M comprises all risky securities in the market, appropriately weighted by their market capitalisation (that is the companies with more outstanding equity in the market will be taking up a bigger proportion of M than those with less quoted equity).

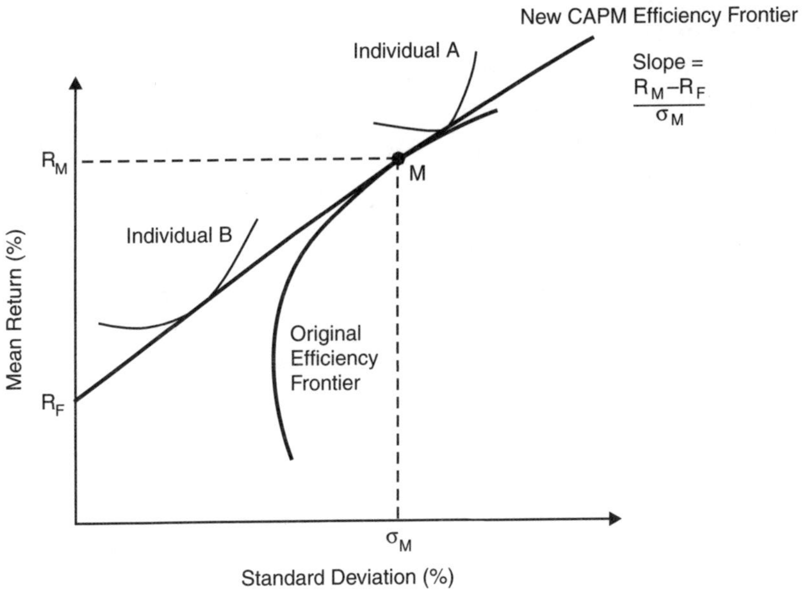

Figure 2.6 The Market Price of Risk

The return on the market is denoted by R_M and the risk-free rate by R_F. Similarly the volatility of the portfolio M is denoted σ_M.

The crucial point of having a linear efficiency frontier which is the same for all individuals is that we can now see that our two investors, who previously chose different equity portfolios depending on their utility functions, will now choose the same equity portfolio (M). What distinguishes the two investors now is how much of M they hold and how much of the riskless asset. In CAPM, there is one unique portfolio, the index of all risky assets, which all individuals will hold regardless of their attitude to risk.

After much thought, Tom decides to ring back Jonathan. He is still not completely sure what to do. CAPM seems so convincing. Yet Tom had not completely forgotten Markowitz either. What do you think he should do? Actually when Markowitz was asked the same question relating to a lump sum pension entitlement he is reputed to have said that while he thought he should have gone out and calculated his individual efficiency frontier, he decided that since existing theories including his own were imperfect, he decided to put 50:50 into bonds and equities and leave it at that! In contrast, Sharpe would presumably have either kept the cash or put some into an equity index fund. Tom likewise decides he has no alternative but to buy some of the index fund Jeremy is recommending. However, rather than putting all his remaining cash into the fund, he decides to keep \$10 000 safely in the bank account for a rainy day. As the bank account is paying the same rate as Treasury bills, for Tom this is more or less equivalent to the riskless asset of CAPM.

Jonathan is neither elated nor over-dismayed by Tom's decision. The large 5% commission on the deal will just pay for his flight on his forthcoming ski weekend in Zermatt with his beautiful new Scandinavian girlfriend which was the objective of calling Tom in the first place, but he had rather hoped that if Tom had gone for more of the index fund, he would have been able to buy his more-steady and equally-attractive Latin American date an expensive ring for Valentine's day. Brokers will break hearts! Resigned to the fact that his girlfriend will just have to wait for that ring, Jonathan heads down to the wine bar to crack a bottle of champagne for having brought a new client to the broking firm. Several bottles later, Jonathan's colleague Chris (known as 'terminator' to his friends because of his ruthless market making) hits on an idea. 'Look,' says Chris 'this guy Tom reads a lot, that's clear from all this stuff he talked to you about CAPM. Why don't we send him some fundamental research on that new aeroplane components stock we're recommending? It is only a very small part of the index but we can tell him it is the undiscovered story of the century and he must have a few more in his portfolio. With the prospective doubling of demand for airline travel over the coming years, these components companies are going to mushroom! Maybe that way we can get the rest of his money!'

Next morning, Tom wakes up to find a special-delivery research note on a little-known Norwegian stock called 'Autopilot' in the post. An hour later Jonathan is on the phone—Tom you have got to buy some of this. Tom's immediate reply is that he does already own some indirectly through the index fund, but Jonathan persists—index funds are for wimps! The real players go for individual stocks. Tom says he will ring back next day after he has had a chance to read the research note. With Jonathan fobbed off at least temporarily, Tom goes back to his book on CAPM to see if he can find any guidance.

There he revisits one of the fundamental points of CAPM—the investor's utility depends on the mean and standard deviation of his total wealth. In considering a new investment opportunity, what matters to the investor is how this will affect his overall mean and standard deviation of wealth. As in all finance, it is the incremental impact of the new asset on total utility that determines its value.

We have already seen this indirectly in our discussion of portfolio theory—remember we simply could not add the individual standard deviations to arrive at the total portfolio standard deviation because the returns on the different stocks would in many cases be correlated, giving the scope for diversification gains—but because this point is crucial, it is worth emphasising in a slightly different way to drive the point home.

Suppose, for example, it is just prior to summer and an investor who lives in Scotland is considering purchasing two shares, one of an ice-cream company called Inverness Ice, and one of a whisky distillery called Glen Glow. Again, to make life simple suppose that with each share only one of two things can happen depending on the state of the world that emerges next month. Think of the two possible states of the world as being one beautiful summer month with lots of sunshine, or an equally horrible month with lots of rain. Shares in Inverness Ice will either be worth £10 or £0 one month from now depending on the weather and exactly the opposite for Glen Glow. If the weather is good, everyone heads out and buys ice cream; if however it is wet, everyone will makes for the bar!

In terms of the framework we developed with Markowitz, these two shares are perfectly negatively correlated (look back to Figure 2.1). Assume, again only for simplicity, that the weather odds are 50:50 according to the local meteorological office. Hence the expected value of each asset is £5. Imagine now you can buy one share but not both. Then, if you are risk averse, you would be willing to pay much less than £5 for either share (a risk averse person will prefer the certainty of £5 in his pocket to the chance of £5). However, suppose now you can hold both assets together. Then if you hold one share of each, you will receive £10 whatever outcome happens (refer again to Figure 2.1 if you are unsure on this point). Hence for both assets you would be prepared to pay up to almost £10 valuing each share at £5!

This example shows clearly how the value of an asset depends not just on that asset's risk characteristics but more generally on how that risk interacts with other assets which the investor can hold. The measure that CAPM uses to assess the risk of an asset relative to the risk of the overall market portfolio is called the *beta* of the stock and is always denoted by the Greek letter β. A β of 1 implies a stock is equally as risky as the market—when the market rises/falls 10%, such a stock will itself on average rise/fall 10%; a β of greater than 1 means a stock is more volatile than the market—when the stock market rises/falls 10%, this stock falls will on average rise/fall more than 10%; finally a β less than 1 means a stock that tends to rise/fall less than the overall market.

As we already know the risk of the market from our earlier analysis (see Figure 2.6), it is straightforward to reach the central result of CAPM. That is simply that the expected return on any stock will equal the risk free rate of interest plus a premium. For a stock that has a β of one, in line with the market, the premium will be exactly the same as the market premium. For a stock that has a β of less than one or more than one, we simply multiply the relevant β by the market premium to obtain the required risk premium for that particular stock. To give an idea of the numbers, historical analysis reveals that the market risk premiums tend to vary from between around 3% for developed markets to anything up to 8% for undeveloped markets. The risk premium for the UK market is normally estimated at around 3%, the Spanish stock market, for example, exhibits a risk premium of nearer 5%, and in some of the Latin American markets the number is up to 8%. Let us say that interest rates in Spain were 5% and we were looking at a required return on a stock that had a historically estimated β of 0.5. From the above analysis it is straightforward to conclude that the required return on this stock will be 7.5%, that is the 5% risk free rate plus a premium of half that of the Spanish market. The interested reader who would like a formal derivation of this result is referred to Box 2.3.

Displaying this graphically for the whole stock market

we have what is referred to as the securities markets line (Figure 2.7). This plots expected returns on stocks as a function of β.

The underlying rationale for the CAPM prediction that expected returns are related to β and not, for example, to the total risk or volatility of the share is that 'non-systematic' risk (that is risk that is related purely to company-specific factors) can be costlessly diversified away by holding a portfolio of stocks. Hence the investor will not receive a return for this diversifiable risk. Instead the investor's return is related to the non-diversifiable risk of the stock as measured by its β.

Tom looked hard at the graph of the securities market line, and then looked at his watch—he could hardly believe how time had flown while he had absorbed the CAPM argument. It was now evening and so he switched on the TV. Slowly a part of Tom's mind became engrossed in the film that was showing—Dr Strangelove—in which the whole drama seemed to reflect a world caught on the dividing line between complexity and order, which just for a

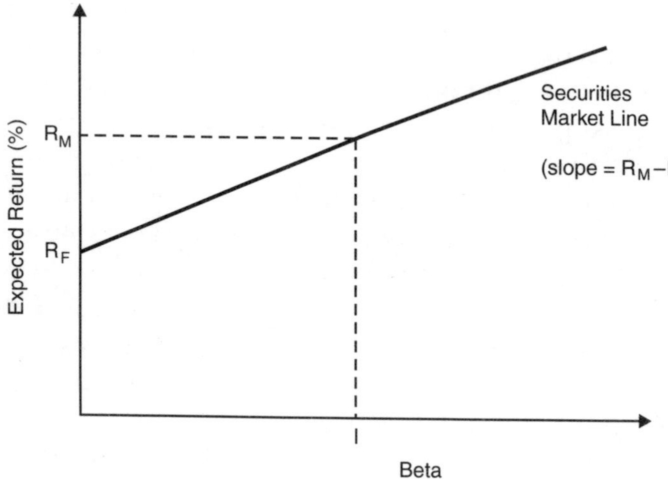

Figure 2.7 The Securities Market Line

Box 2.3 Derivation of CAPM

Once we know the risk of the market, we can easily calculate the risk of any individual stock. Denote the risk of the market by its standard deviation σ_M. Hence to measure the risk of any asset (labelled by subscript i), we simply multiply this figure by the β of the asset in question:

$$\text{Risk of asset } i = \beta_i \sigma_M$$

What about the cost of this risk in any asset? To find this out we simply multiply the total risk of the stock in question by the market price of risk which we already know from our analysis to be the slope for the budget line (remember Figure 2.6). This gives us what is referred to as the risk adjustment for any stock:

$$\text{Risk adjustment} = \beta_i \sigma_M (R_M - R_F)/\sigma_M = \beta_i (R_M - R_F)$$

From here we can move on to the central result of the CAPM. In equilibrium, all assets must earn the same risk-adjusted return (otherwise arbitrageurs would buy the shares with the greater risk adjusted return and sell those with the lower risk-adjusted returns—and in so doing iron out the pricing discrepancy). Hence, for example any equity's risk-adjusted return must equal the risk-free rate of interest on the government bond. In symbols:

$$R_i - \beta_i (R_M - R_F) = R_F$$

Rearranging this equation gives the CAPM as it is usually stated:

$$R_i = R_F + \beta_i (R_M - R_F)$$

In words, the expected return on any asset must equal the risk-free rate plus a risk adjustment. Hence for any stock we can calculate its expected return once we have an estimate of its β, if we know the market price of risk and the risk-free rate.

moment Tom thought might have parallels to the world of financial markets. But the other part of Tom's mind was haunted by the apparent rationality of the securities markets line. Soon the TV was off and Tom was in bed for a good night's rest—he needed it after all that reading!

As he lay in the darkness, however, sleep evaded him. Soon the hi-fi was on and the background was Paul Simon's 'The only living boy in New York'. The line 'half of the time we're gone, but we don't know where' kept echoing in Tom's mind as he grappled with the concepts in CAPM. Slowly it dawned on him that what Jonathan had actually proposed to him was that there was a stock whose return, adjusted for risk, was greater than what he could get from a risk-free bond, or from the index fund. According to Jonathan, there was a way to beat the market by finding securities with a risk/return trade-off lying above the securities market line. According to CAPM, however, such mis-pricing was either transient or illusory. There is no way to beat the market and the best an investor can do is to distribute his wealth according to his risk preferences between the Index fund and the risk-free rate of interest. Either Jonathan did not know what he was talking about, or else he had discovered a market inefficiency in the pricing of risk that was likely to disappear. He would have to be quick.

Next morning, Tom moved into the racy world of finance with his final \$10 000 going into the aeroplane components stock. Little did Tom realise that he had been sold the stock off Chris' market-making book at a 50% profit to the broking firm. Jonathan cracked another bottle of champagne and his Latin American girlfriend got that ring after all! (Two years later, however, she melted it down during a surge in the gold price—remember Chapter 1!)

FURTHER DEVELOPMENTS OF CAPM

Armed with the theory of CAPM and the hint that the Holy

Grail of Finance had finally been unearthed in the Ivory Towers rather than down in Wall Street, in the 1970s the academics wasted no time in trying to do poor brokers and fund managers out of a job for good. The line of attack was a straight attempt at destruction of anything other than the 'market portfolio' approach to investment. Now was the chance to prove that you might as well get the kids to throw darts at the relevant pages of the *Wall Street Journal* or the *Financial Times* rather than paying over the odds for the advice of your private banker, fund manager or broker like Jonathan who was always impossible to find anyway, dashing around from one exotic holiday to the next, purportedly on the mission to find the next 'undiscovered' stock or market.

Computer models were cranked furiously in an effort to confirm that, yes, companies with low βs did indeed have low average returns and high share prices (risk-averse investors will be eager to buy low β shares whose inclusion in a portfolio will reduce overall portfolio risk and vice-versa for high β shares (Figure 2.8). In other words, the evidence appeared to show that stock markets correctly reflect the relevant underlying company fundamentals in respect of expected returns and risk characteristics as measured by β. One inference to be drawn from these studies was that individuals were not able to systematically use information to pick winners. This information was already embedded in prices. There simply was no way to consistently beat the market (see Box 2.4 for a discussion of the relationship between this result and Efficient Markets Theory).

TRACKER FUNDS

Against the background of the previous section, it is hardly surprising that portfolio indexing got off the ground in earnest. Index funds were initially set up in the US (the first equity fund was launched by Wells Fargo in 1971), and

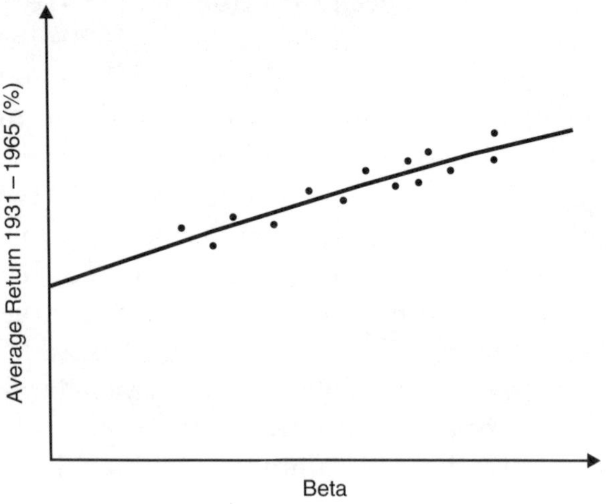

Figure 2.8 Empirical Studies of β

Source: Black, Jenson, Scholes (1972) in Jenson (ed.) *Studies in the Theory of Capital Markets*

today almost 35% of institutional investment is in the form of such funds. The UK followed several years later and today approaching 20% of British institutional money is tied up in index funds of one sort or another, with much more 'quasi-indexed', meaning that the actual proportions of the portfolio invested in different stocks and indices are only marginally different from index weightings. While one does, occasionally, hear of cases of the revenge of the active manager (for example in the UK in August 1998, Barclays Global Investors, a committed and respected indexing specialist, lost two mandates from an insurance company and a pension fund worth over £400 million to active rivals), the trend is still clearly in the opposite direction, with a total of over £10 billion in 1998 alone in the UK moving from active to passive management.

What is perhaps even more disturbing for the active fund management case is that there is increasing evidence of

Box 2.4 CAPM and Efficient Markets Theory

The analysis of risk and return embodied in CAPM is sometimes confused with what is referred to as the Efficient Markets Hypothesis (EMH). This is unfortunate but perhaps understandable since both approaches are popularly summed up by saying 'you cannot beat the market'. However, the two models are conceptually different and address different questions. CAPM is a model of stock price valuation, purporting to predict securities' returns as a function of β as we have seen in the text. EMH, on the other hand, is a model of the dynamics (changes over time) of share prices, and could in principle be compatible with various models of asset valuation (of which CAPM is but one example).

EMH has its roots in the analysis of French commodities markets by Louis Bachelier as long ago as 1890. Bachelier tried to rationalise why such prices appeared to follow a 'random walk' over time. The term 'random walk' refers to successive price changes which are independent of one another. In other words, if a share price random walks, then the price change between today and tomorrow (and hence tomorrow's price) cannot be predicted by looking at the price change between yesterday and today. Just as it can be proven that the best place to find an inebriate student left lying on the beach (St. Andrews) or the Common (Oxford) is where the student was originally abandoned, so the best estimate of tomorrow's commodity price, following Bachelier, is simply today's price. Both drunkards and commodities follow a random walk, as likely to go one way as the other.

The EMH model is commonly applied to the analysis of share price movements as well. Given an initial equilibrium share price (perhaps but not necessarily determined by β), share price movements will be related to 'news' on the company and the economy. While news may be either good or bad, it will certainly be independent of the last piece of information and hence the share price will random walk, as likely to go up (good news) as down (bad news). EMH is often further developed to distinguish how quickly different pieces of news become reflected in prices and in particular three categories are common in the literature: weak efficiency (share prices reflect all information imbedded in historic prices—or if you like the market does not suffer from memory lapses); semi-strong-efficiency (the share price of a company reflects all publicly available information relating to that company such as industry forecasts and brokers' reports, in addition to the company's own reports and announcements); and strong efficiency (share prices reflect all information—including insider or non-public information.

The EMH model is sometimes used itself as a justification for portfolio indexing, but this is misleading. It may be a justification for a passive approach to investment (especially in its strong form), but this does not imply that all individuals should then simply buy an index fund—rather it returns us to the world of Markowitz where each individual is free to choose his own optimal portfolio dependent on his attitude towards risk.

metamorphosis in some of the bigger active funds, as they become increasingly like index funds. At the time of writing, Fidelity's Magellan Fund, the supposed paragon of an active stock picking fund, has as six of its top ten holdings the same stocks as the Vanguard S&P 500 index fund! At the same time, Fidelity's Contrafund, whose stated investment objective is 'to invest in companies whose value is not fully recognised by the public' has Microsoft as one of its top holdings! There almost seems to be a Darwinian mechanism at work to weed out the active funds by hook or by crook!

However, the attempt to index a portfolio has some initial problems. First of all, one has the obvious question of which index to choose. Presumably, to reflect as far as possible the overall market for risky assets, one should choose as broad an index as possible. That rules out some of the older indices in the mature markets such as the Dow Jones (US), and the FT 30 (UK) each of which is composed of only thirty shares. However, if one attempts to index a portfolio to broader indices in these markets, say the S&P 500 in the US (comprising as the name suggests five hundred shares) or the FT All Share Index in the UK (comprising over eight hundred shares), there is a formidable number of shares which the index fund must track.

In practice full replication of a broad index can be both difficult and uneconomic, considering the tedious administration associated with dividend distributions, rights issues, changes to the constituents of the index etc. Costs associated with these issues infer that an index fund which truly aims to replicate a given index will inevitably 'under-perform' given that these costs must be absorbed by the fund.

To circumvent such problems, most actual index trackers use sampling approaches. Rather than investing in all the stocks in a particular index, a hopefully representative group of the stocks is chosen. This will certainly include the largest shares in the index, but beyond that, a few stocks will be chosen from each sector with a view to capturing the major movements in each of these sectors. However, a 'tracking error' is inevitable, again applying costs to the investor who truly wants to hold the 'market portfolio'. These tracking errors can be particularly important in emerging markets funds, where replication is hampered by the enhanced volatility which is a characteristic of these markets. In fact in 1998 Barclays Global Investors lost a £200m emerging markets mandate to rival State Street precisely over an argument over what constitutes an excessive tracking error in such markets.

A further problem is that even these larger and better-known indices can trap the unwary investor in unanticipated ways. Most of the more common share indices around the world, for example, do not include dividends in their estimate of portfolio returns (because they are only trying to track short-term performance), but the DAX in Germany, for example, does include dividends in its estimate of the portfolio returns accruing to the thirty shares that make up that index. But even these subtleties pale into insignificance when one considers the strange case of another popular index, the Nikkei 225. This, as its name suggests consists of two hundred and twenty five shares in the Japanese stock market. What the name does not tell us however, is the weird and wonderful construction of the index. The first of the traps for the unwary investor is the fact that it is unweighted, calculated (more or less) by adding up the individual share prices and dividing by two hundred and twenty five. That implies that an industrial conglomerate such as Mitsubishi Heavy industries, or electronics giant Toshiba, for example, both of which have many billions of dollars in annual sales, have the same weight in the index as the smallest stock by market capitalisation, the little-known Shimura Kako, a specialist nickel employer with sales of under $100 million! But the anomalies of the Nikkei 225 do not stop there. Japan's second-largest retailer, Ito-Yokado, one of the top-ten stocks by market capitalisation in Japan, is not in the index. Neither is the large banking group, Industrial Bank of Japan, despite the fact that smaller banking groups do appear in the index. Confused? You are not alone!

But even if we accept the indexing paradigm and try to find solutions as best we can to the above technical problems, there is a further and more complex technical problem with jumping to the conclusion that putting one's money into an index fund is the best combination of risk and return available on the capital markets. That problem is as follows. The market portfolio in CAPM is a hybrid portfolio theoretically embracing all risky assets available in the market place, including not just shares, bonds, and other similar financial instruments both domestic and international, but also real assets such as art and antiques, to name but two examples, and also potentially intangible assets such as education. To jump from the conclusions of CAPM to investing one's money all in an index fund is to miss the point that diversification within one asset class such as equities is likely to be substantially inferior to diversification between asset classes, especially between financial and non-financial assets. And yet often this point is missed. The result is that an investor who limits his exposure to risk by buying an available equity index fund in the market will be incorrectly diversified, even in a CAPM sense, not just because that index will almost inevitably not comprise every available equity, but because potentially superior portfolios comprising other classes of asset exist. By definition such portfolios have to be 'hand made' rather than being available to buy off the shelf.

CONCLUSIONS

Our journey through portfolio theory has yielded some interesting insights. First of all, while the portfolio theory of Markowitz does suggest that a passive approach to fund management is appropriate, it does not suggest that such an approach necessarily implies portfolio indexing—rather that each individual should tailor his portfolio to his own risk preferences. However, the stronger set of assumptions underlying CAPM does lead to the view that passive portfolio indexing, properly interpreted to mean investing in an index comprising all the risky assets available in the market place, is the optimal investment strategy for an investor wanting exposure to risk. CAPM apparently solves the asset allocation and stock selection problem at one fell swoop. Investors should simply index their portfolios and thereby achieve the best risk/return combination which the stock market has to offer. While this investment strategy is neither a recipe to avoid disasters or to enjoy exceptional gains, on average it will come out best: 'you cannot beat it so you had better join it' is the message.

3

Difficulties—Financial Markets in the Full Light of Day

INTRODUCTION

While at the practical level the 'market portfolio' approach to asset management has grown ever stronger since the early 1970s, back in the universities subsequent generations of finance specialists have been quietly becoming increasingly concerned at the uncritical acceptance of the dominant CAPM paradigm. These worries began with empirical studies which suggested that either βs had only a partial role in explaining observed share returns, or worse still, in some studies, that they had no role at all in explaining such returns! But if β fails to encapsulate the uncertainty of a share, the theoretical case for portfolio indexing is lost. Indeed, a full re-examination of CAPM reveals substantial questions on which the model is silent but which lie at the heart of financial market dynamics. When we look closely at these issues, the weakness of portfolio indexing as a strategy becomes all too evident.

These more central challenges are that the CAPM seems

completely unable to capture at least three important realities in financial markets. The first is that information is not complete nor is it distributed evenly in financial markets, even in 'developed' rather than 'emerging' markets. This attacks head on the risk framework underlying CAPM, including the assumptions of full and evenly distributed information with well-defined probabilities attached to events. The second is that the investment universe is strategic with market participants interacting through their attempts to outguess each other. This challenges the 'parametric' framework underlying CAPM and substantially complicates the definition and meaning of rationality embedded in the market model. The third feature of financial markets is that investment decisions are not 'once for all' as in CAPM but that such decisions are made sequentially over time. Again, this has important implications for both strategy and rationality which CAPM side-steps. In short, information uncertainties, strategic intrigue and timing are all important aspects in understanding capital market dynamics. Although these issues are intricately linked together as practising investors will realise, a lot is to be learned by examining them separately. Then in the penultimate section we bring them together to see that the overall implication is that these features prevent arbitrageurs from doing their work. Without arbitrage, markets can stray from the equilibrium for protracted periods of time, exhibiting 'hysteresis' effects and the sorts of booms and crashes we are well aware of from the media. In such a world, the theoretical case for market indexing *à la* CAPM is non-existent.

THE LIMITATIONS OF THE RISK FRAMEWORK FOR ANALYSING UNCERTAINTY

With regard to the risk framework, challenges can be levelled from several directions. The crucial one, in my view, relates to the assumption of full information evenly distributed amongst market participants (for an introduction to further lines of attack see Box 3.1). This assumption lies at the heart of CAPM. In practical terms it requires us to believe that all investors, both buyers and sellers, have full knowledge about share returns as summarised by their expected returns and volatility of returns. However in actual

Box 3.1 Other Problems with the Risk Framework

Readers will note that I have chosen to concentrate on the problems of imperfect information for CAPM in the main text. This is because I consider this theme to be the really crucial issue concerning the risk framework underlying CAPM. However, more academic approaches to the subject will also spend time detailing some of the problems concerned with the utility functions underlying portfolio analysis and CAPM, and in particular some of the problems associated with the expected utility rule. To give you a flavour of some of this dissident work, consider the following simple example of a possible problem associated with the expected utility rule, sometimes referred to as the Ellsberg Paradox (but be careful—in his work Ellsberg detailed other paradoxes as well).

Bag 1 has fifty red balls and fifty black balls in it. Bag 2 has one hundred red and black balls but the proportions are unknown. First question. Which bet would you prefer—to bet on a red ball being drawn from Bag 1 or to bet on a Red ball being drawn from Bag 2. In experiments it appears that most people prefer to bet on a red ball being drawn from Bag 1 over the bet of a red ball being drawn from Bag 2. However, second question. Which bet would you prefer—to bet on a black ball being drawn from Bag 1 or to bet on a black ball being drawn from Bag 2. In experiments many people also seem to prefer the bet of a black ball being drawn from Bag 1 over a Black ball being drawn from Bag 2. Yet this is in violation of the expected utility rule since if we prefer the Bag 1 on the red bet, that infers we should prefer Bag 2 on the black bet.

markets there are at least two major problems which CAPM fails to address. The first is the reality that there may well be nuggets of information known to buyers but unknown to sellers and even more likely *vice versa*. Such asymmetries can radically alter the workings of markets as we shall see. The second problem is the heroic leap involved in reducing the uncertainty inherent in investment decisions to the statistical concept of probability and risk. Where the world is less clear than this, however, we can again observe markets working in rather different ways than CAPM would suggest.

Asymmetric Information and Markets Playing Tricks

A good way to come to grips with the problems for financial markets when information is distributed unevenly is to begin with an analysis of insurance markets. Insurance companies pool independent risks from large numbers of people with a view to being able to offer individuals attractive terms under which these individuals can give themselves at least some protection to their income and wealth in the event of some pre-specified undesired event such as a car accident, a home fire, an illness etc. The key to the deal is the independence of each individual's particular risk. Life insurance companies do not know, for example, which of their policy holders will die in a particular year, but they have a very good idea of the proportion of their policy holders that will die in that same year. They also know that, in general, any one policy holder's death will not have implications for the life or death of other policy holders. This allows the insurance company to take in relatively small premiums from all its clients and to offer a much larger sum to dependants of policy holders that die, while continuing to earn a profit for its shareholders. Yet insurance companies have long been aware of at least two structural problems with offering insurance policies (for a historical discussion see Box 3.2).

Box 3.2 Insurance, Lloyd's of London and Information Asymmetries

The latter half of the seventeenth century saw a flourishing of interest in insurance matters. In 1693, Edmund Halley (of comet fame) published a set of life expectancy tables that laid the foundations for Britain's life assurance industry. His paper was subsequently revised by a Kent Preacher called Richard Price and sold to the Equitable Society to assist it in its ability to set premiums for life insurance and annuities. Alas, as with much pioneering work, some faults lay in Price's analysis. In fact he underestimated life expectancies with the result that life premiums were higher than they needed to be. This led to healthy profits for the Equitable Society but the British Government, using the same tables to determine annuity payments to its pensioners, lost heavily!

At around the same time, in 1687 to be exact, Edward Lloyd opened a coffee shop near the River Thames on Tower Street where merchants from the ships moored at London Docks gathered, exchanging notes on the hazards at sea and seeking insurance for their various voyages. The coffee, the chat and the business proved so popular that in 1691 Lloyd moved the shop to new spacious quarters in Lombard Street, and in 1696, he launched 'Lloyd's List', a detailed record on ship movements provided by a set of correspondents in Britain and the Continent. The publication became so prestigious that even the government used it to publish the latest news of its various sea battles.

In 1771, nearly one hundred years after the opening of the coffee shop on Tower Street, seventy nine of the underwriters who did business at Lloyd's each subscribed £100 and formed the Society of Lloyd's, an unincorporated group with potentially limitless liability. The members, or 'Names' as they were subsequently called, pledged all their earthly possessions and all their financial capital to make good their customers losses. For over 200 years, Lloyd's was the most famous of all insurance companies until infamy set in during the 1990s with a series of damaging asbestos and other environmental claims threatening to leave some Names penniless and to undermine the whole basis of Lloyd's insurance. The overall issue involved Names claiming that agents were underwriting risks without any proper understanding of the uncertainties involved and without proper disclosure, is a classic example within the insurance world of the theme of this chapter.

The first is the adverse selection problem. Let us assume that smoking negatively affects life expectancy, an hypothesis for which there is compelling if not conclusive evidence. For a life assurance company, however, it is practically impossible to know which of its potential clients are smokers and those who are not. The true underlying characteristics of buyers, and in particular their propensity to smoke, are difficult for the sellers of life assurance to observe prior to signing the contract. All that the life company can observe is the average population behaviour. Imagine the company offers a life premium based on average mortality rates. Non-smokers, with above-average life expectancy rates, will find the premium to be over-expensive; smokers, however, will realise they are on to a good thing and are effectively being offered a subsidy at the expense of non-smokers. The net result is that the market is in danger of selecting the bad risks with smokers queuing up for cover, while the good risks cannot obtain cover at a fair price. Such a situation can in the extreme lead to the disappearance of the market.

The second problem is that of moral hazard. With your house fully insured, what incentive have you to bother locking up when you go out, especially if you feel it is time to replace your hi-fi anyway? Here the seller of the insurance faces the problem of not being able to have full information on the actions of the buyer after writing the insurance contract. If the act of insuring increases the likelihood of the event insured against happening, the problem is referred to as one of moral hazard. Again severe moral hazard can threaten to lead to the disappearance of the market.

While asymmetric information amongst market participants can lead to complete market collapse, more often it leads to the possibility of opportunistic and monopolistic behaviour by certain market members within an imperfect market. Such behaviour can wreak havoc not just in insurance markets but more generally in other financial markets. To get a feeling of just how serious these problems can be in stock markets, think of the new issue market for equity finance, especially in the smaller company segment of the market, and the potential problem of adverse selection. Many buyers of new issues in smaller companies effectively consider them as one asset class, even more so in emerging markets where detailed prospectuses may be unavailable. All investors can know with any certainty is the average return from investing in these issues. Of course the sellers of these issues, the managers of the companies themselves, are usually well aware of the true quality of the underlying company which they manage. But if such issues are priced at the average valuation for such issues at the time, trouble is in store with 'badly managed' companies having the incentive to issue equity at the prevailing average valuation for such companies, while good management teams cannot get finance on fair terms. This 'false' pricing can have dramatic implications for markets.

Perhaps the most classic example of a related phenomenon to the above in financial markets is the story of the events associated with the South Sea Company in the early eighteenth century. A company was set up under monopoly licence by a group of Tories to sell British goods to people in South America by barter, in return for the exotic goods from the South Seas. However, the monopoly licence carried a cost; the company agreed to take on just under £10 million of unfunded public debt which had been largely accumulated by the colourful but bellicose William of Orange. In effect the company had two divisions; a trading arm and a financial arm. Unfortunately the latter dominated the former. An ambitious scheme launched by the company in 1720 aimed to refinance over £30 million of government debt in private hands at a lower rate of interest, by persuading existing holders of the debt to swap their bonds for equity in the South Sea Company. The state would owe the South Sea Company a debt equivalent to that converted, but at a lower rate of interest.

As everyone who has ever had any experience in mergers and acquisitions will be aware, the trick, of course, was in the conversion price. The nominal capital of the South Sea Company increased by the nominal amount of the debt exchanged. For example, for every £100 of South Sea stock issued for £100 of government stock, the company's share capital increased by £100. But if shares of nominal value £100 were valued in the market at a premium, say, £200, then for the same issue of new shares, not only could the company buy the outstanding state debt but it would also potentially receive a substantial cash injection to boost its funds. And this is exactly what the company's fraudulent directors did, 'hyping' the share with a series of marketing ploys and false promises to at one stage over £1000 per share, sucking in investors such as Sir Issac Newton along the way. Market interest in the project generated over one hundred other bubble companies to come to the market. Some, such as the future Sun Insurance company, were *bona fide* enterprises, but many others, each with its own alchemic recipe for instant riches, including the South Sea Company, were not.

However, not everyone was fooled by the ruse. The stock analysts of the day were obviously the poets (perhaps it would be better if they still were!), including Alexander Pope who had enough foresight to write before the South Sea bubble broke:

Ye wise philosophers! Explain
What magick makes our money rise

When dropt into the southern Main;
Or do these jugglers cheat our Eyes?

Of course, Pope was right—the jugglers were no more than the players on Yeats' painted stage. When the bubble burst, investors were left penniless. Of the many famous quotes of those unfortunate investors, the one by Sir Issac Newton, sums up not just his despair but encapsulates perfectly one of the themes of this book:

'I can calculate the motions of the heavenly bodies, but not the madness of people.'

Poor Sir Issac had sold his original holding at a 100% profit, but seeing the share rise further, had re-entered the fray in a moment's insanity. The gravity of the crowd had proved too much to resist!

However, investors may want to reflect that even adverse selection is not all bad news for the new issues market. Good companies may be unable to raise money, but at least when the market 'disappears', the unscrupulous cannot fool investors any longer. Amongst companies that never made it to the market after the South Sea Bubble were such gems as 'For the better curing of Venereal Disease' and best of all 'A company for carrying on an undertaking of great advantage, but nobody to know what it is'!

But the problems of asymmetric information and stock bubbles are, alas, not just confined to the history books. A modern example is the so-called Bre-X scandal. In 1996, shares in Bre-X, a Canadian gold-prospecting company, reached $284 a share on news of a significant prospective gold find in Borneo, Indonesia. Less than a year later the shares were suspended at below $3 a share, as the company sought bankruptcy protection. What had gone wrong?

Perhaps we shall never know the final truth, but it is certain that the root cause was asymmetrically-distributed information in the marketplace. The likely chain of events started with the local Bre-X geologist Michael de Guzman buying about 60 ounces of river gold from local tribesmen and then staging a $6bn dollar fraud by mixing the metal with crushed rocks, apparently achieved on top of a pool table! These 'samples' were then sent as proof of his claim to have found the largest ever individual gold field, and were sufficiently convincing to dupe Bre-X Vice Chairman and Chief Geologist John Felderhof and CEO David Walsh (at least this is one version of the story; another view includes Felderhof and Walsh in the plot).

Only when joint-venture partner Freeport McMorans due diligence test showed negligible amounts of gold on the site and further independent tests confirmed this latter result did the full extent of the scandal break. By then de Guzman, Felderhof and Walsh were multimillionaires having cashed in options during the stock's halcyon days. De Guzman subsequently died when he fell from a helicopter in an apparent suicide. Felderhof, denying any involvement in the affair, headed off to Grand Cayman and to his luxury villa acquired with some of the booty. David Walsh, a reputed chain-smoker even before the scandal started to unfold, simply bought as many cartons as he could find in Calgary and locked himself up in his office to try to sort out the legal implications of the mess. Nesbitt Burns Inc., the Bank of Montreal's broking arm, claimed with some justification that it had been victimised as a $3bn lawsuit was filed by investors against it and its star gold-mining analyst Egizio Bianchini, who had been bullish on the stock before the crash. Alas poor Egizio was not a poet!

Problems of asymmetric information and skulduggery such as that involved in the Bre-X scandal are not just to be found in the far-off climes of the Indonesian jungle. The problems can appear much nearer to home in perfectly developed markets. Polly Peck International was a FTSE 100 company whose equity was valued by the London Stock Market at over £1.5bn in the summer of 1990. Its main businesses were food and electronics which had both grown substantially through acquisition in 1989 (the former through the acquisition of US group Del Monte; the latter through the acquisition of a majority stake in the Japanese group Sansui). The first half 1990 interim results and balance sheet had apparently shown borrowings of around £800m to be offset to a material degree by cash of £400m. This left net gearing (that is borrowings minus cash, all divided by equity) at just under 100%, a high but not outrageous ratio for a company where at least one of its businesses (food) was relatively defensive to any economic turndown.

However, on September 20th, 1990, Polly Peck's share plunged over 50% to 108p and a month later the company was placed into administration. Subsequently the company's chairman, Mr Asil Nadir, who had been due to face charges of theft at the Old Bailey (London's Central Criminal Court), jumped bail and fled the country, in the tradition of fraudsters going back as far as Robert Knight, one of the swindlers of the South Sea bubble we have already discussed.

And just to put a final nail in the coffin to anyone that believes that such events are the exception rather than the rule in equity markets, two examples which emerged over the weeks that this particular section of *Portfolio Indexing* was being written. The first was Alcatel, the French engineering and telecommunications group, whose shares fell 36% on September 17th 1998, recording the biggest ever fall in the history of the Paris stock exchange. The reason? The official explanation was an unexpected profits warning that the company's full year operating profits would be well below analyst expectations because of investment cuts among telecom operators and the downturn in the Far East. However seasoned investors were left to speculate that surely such information must have been known by the company for some time. The Asian crisis was already a year old! Why did the warning not come earlier? A suspicious mind might wonder if it could possibly have been anything to do with an acquisition of a specialist switch company called DSC in the

US, an acquisition that was paid for in Alcatel shares? Former owners of DSC certainly thought so, and at the moment of writing various law suits are pending! Re-read the South Sea bubble story about the importance of the exchange ratio in debt/equity and equity/equity swaps!

Meanwhile in a set of events that eventually was to lead to his resignation, Gian Mario Rossignolo, the Chairman of Telecom Italia, one of Italy's three largest companies by market capitalisation and the fourth largest telecom group in Europe, had to face angry shareholders when his share price fell 22% over a ten day period on the back of a news leak, initially denied but then confirmed, which suggested profits would be less than expected. Attempts to fob off the leak, on the grounds that the profits warning was designed to help management in an expected confrontation over pay with unions, failed to reassure shareholders and eventually Rossignolo had to go. Investors could not believe that such information had been withheld for a protracted period. Yet another example of the bubbles in markets and share prices which asymmetric information can generate.

So far the discussion has focused on implications of asymmetric information in securities markets. What about the other problem we discussed in insurance markets, that is moral hazard? Has this implications for securities markets as well?

The answer is that moral hazard problems can lead to just as great, if not even greater problems in financial markets. Moral hazard potentially affects equity markets indirectly through the credit and money markets. Major central banks of the world, including the Fed, traditionally have assumed a 'lender of last resort' role, being prepared to step in to aid ailing banks that run into liquidity problems. That in itself can create a problem—if managers of banks know that they will be bailed out of any potential crisis, might they not have the incentive to engage in riskier lending than might otherwise be prudent and to go for broke? Perversely the attempts by governments to make financial systems more secure might be the very thing that makes them more dangerous. Automatic federal deposit insurance was a key part of the demise of many savings and loans institutions in the US in the late 1980s for just this reason. In fact since 1970 there have been seventy (yes seventy) banking crises in the global economy, not just in the emergent markets of Cote D'Ivoire or Senegal, for example, but also in the UK, Japan, Scandinavia, Spain and, as we have seen, the US itself, purportedly the world's most sophisticated and best regulated financial system. In many of these cases the underlying cause was moral hazard and there was a direct spillover onto equity markets not just as the shares of the banks concerned were quoted, but indirectly via the recessions that ensued in the domestic economies.

Further and perhaps more worryingly, international institutions such as the International Monetary Fund are increasingly playing an international lender of last resort role in the global economy, standing by to pump money into economies that have run into serious international payments difficulties. The Mexican crisis which we shall examine in Chapter 4 produced a quantum leap in the scale of IMF activity in emerging markets, being part of a syndicate that put together a \$50bn 'bail out' package to allow Mexico to repay creditors that had made dollar loans to the country. But the obvious question arises as to whether such aid might not in part have fuelled the East Asian crisis that erupted two years later. By arranging for the bail out of creditors—mainly foreign financial institutions—surely the IMF in fact encouraged the very same institutions to play the same game in other emerging markets. The spillover effects in each case to equities markets were dramatic, again as we shall see in Chapter 4. This is the underlying danger with the decision taken late in 1998 to further increase the resources of the IMF for dealing with financial crises—maybe all that is happening is that the stakes are being increased every time but one day there will be a reckoning!

Incomplete Information and Irreducible Uncertainty

Unfortunately, we have just scratched the surface in terms of the real-world problems in financial markets with these examples of the problems arising with asymmetric information. Notice that the defining characteristic of these problems was not incomplete information looking at all the market participants as one group but rather that different segments of the market had different pieces of information with little or no incentive to share it. The pieces of the jigsaw are all there, it is just that different people have different pieces.

A further problem arises when information is incomplete or in the extreme non-existent. Here pieces of the jigsaw are actually missing, creating potentially major gaps in our knowledge. In the world of securities markets, incomplete information is the norm rather than the exception as we are involved in assessing future events about which we often have little knowledge or understanding. The fact is that investment decisions are often shrouded in such mystery as to fall well beyond the possibility of being summarised by a few statistical measures of risk. It was no less than John Maynard Keynes, one of the best-known economists of the twentieth century, who started his analysis of the investment decision by emphasising the precariousness of the basis of knowledge on which our estimates of prospective returns have to be made. He sums it up as follows:

'If we speak frankly, we have to admit that our basis of knowledge for estimating the yield ten years hence of a railway, a copper mine, a textile factory, the goodwill of a patent medicine, an Atlantic liner, a building in the City of London, amounts to little and sometimes to nothing'.

Strong words indeed from someone who had written an influential essay on the theory of statistics and certainly a far cry from the assumptions underlying CAPM. If Keynes' vision is correct, on what basis then does the investment community decide the prospective returns in such diverse sectors of the market as transport, natural resources, industry, pharmaceuticals, shipping and finance!

Of course you may protest that we can still fall back on the Savage method of uncertainty assessment outlined in Chapter 1. Here investors reveal by their very actions their implicit view of the probabilities involved. However, the point is that there is no objective basis for these estimates. As a result, in any particular stock or indeed market investment, some investors will prove to be close to the mark, others will be far from it, while still others will refuse to play what amounts to 'financial blind date'. There are undoubtedly situations under which individuals will be unable to decide rationally which probability beliefs to attach to events because those events are genuinely uncertain. Ignorance does not equal stupidity!

What happens in stock and bond markets when we are in situations of unquantifiable uncertainty? We are then definitely in the world described so clearly in both Charles Kindleberger's classic *Manias, Panics and Crashes* and in Bernice Cohen's *The Edge of Chaos*. Mob psychology and 'following the crowd' syndromes are inevitable. Markets do not signal to us efficient prices but rather their volatility is simply a reflection of short-term sentiment, with waves of excessive optimism followed by currents of equally-excessive pessimism.

To see such uncertainty at work, we need look no further than the financial events associated with the second half of 1998. By September 1998, a sequence of Far Eastern turmoil, Russian debt default, and fears of a Brazilian crash had taken a heavy toll not just on emerging markets globally but on the developed markets of the world as well. No one was quite sure just how severe the deflationary effects on developed economies coming from their emerging neighbours would be. Even Alan Greenspan, Chairman of the Federal Reserve, admitted, with refreshing honesty from a senior establishment figure, in early October 1998 a high degree of uncertainty about the likely denouement, summing up the problem as 'a broad area of uncertainty and fear'. Volatility in even the most solid assets became huge, with the dollar falling at its extreme point by 20% against the yen in a mere three days. There was a major shift from all financial assets, even high quality bonds to cash. Again Greenspan captured the issue perfectly:

'A major shift towards liquidity protection is really not a market phenomenon, it is a fear-induced psychological response'.

What do our discussions above on asymmetric and incomplete information tell us about portfolio indexing? Rather than the CAPM world where indexing guarantees an optimal portfolio strategy, in a world of imperfect information flows portfolio indexing is little, if anything, more than the decision to follow the crowd blindly, and in many cases dangerously. In today's financial markets, β fails to summarise the risk assumed by the investor. The uncertainties are significantly more complex. In CAPM, indexing is like an automatic pilot taking us in the most effective way through the world of risk; in the world of imperfect information, indexing resembles more the decision to allow oneself to be flown in a plane with no pilot, automatic or human.

STRATEGY AND THE COMPLEXITIES OF RATIONALITY

So far we have seen that with informational asymmetries and deficiencies, there is ample scope to explain the phenomena of bubbles and crashes we typically observe in securities markets and more generally for stocks and markets to follow patterns incompatible with fundamentals. This in turn raises questionmarks about portfolio indexing as an optimal investment strategy. However, even if we set aside such difficulties, there is another aspect of financial markets that potentially is equally as important in explaining such features, that is the fact that the investment universe is strategic.

To say that an investment environment is strategic means that it is generally incorrect to assume that investors cannot and do not influence each other's behaviour in making investment decisions. A problem is, as every fund manager knows only too well, the decision environment faced by investors is often not parametric because decisions about what course of action to take involve not only estimations of the value of future variables, but of the actions and hence expectations of other investors. My best action depends on what you think my estimate is of what action you will take; hence my best action depends on what I think you think I think etc. etc. etc. Anyone who has any interest in card games such as poker, or who has industry experience of pricing and other strategic decisions, will immediately identify with the problems that strategic interaction raises.

To return to Keynes, in his *General Theory* he describes the essence of the investment decision as being like a newspaper competition in which the competitors have to pick out the six prettiest faces from one hundred photographs with the prize going to the contestant whose choice nearest corresponds to the average preferences of competitors as a whole. In other words, each competitor has to pick, not those faces which he himself finds prettiest, but those he thinks most likely to catch the fancy of the other competitors, all of whom are looking at the problem from the same point of view! A moment's thought will show that this is another way of expressing the infinite regress problem explained above, as each competitor effectively has to choose not those faces that he himself finds prettiest, nor those that he believes average opinion will find prettiest, but those which he believes average opinion expects average opinion to be prettiest etc.

The essence of the Keynes problem identified here as applied to financial markets is that investors are intractably tied up in a problem of trying to guess what the basis of conventional wisdom will be in the future. A simple example which has been a substantial problem for fund managers in the 1990s is trying to identify what is the conventional valuation standard used by the industry. Is it the price/earnings ratio which has come into increasing question as financial markets have become more geographically integrated but where accounting systems can lead to very different statements of earnings? If not, are price/cash flow ratios of more practical use by eliminating non-cash items which is where the different accounting systems have their greatest effect. The effect on stock selection of choosing one or the other ratio can be dramatic. For example, if price/earnings is still the more widely used standard, to select companies on the basis of low price/cash flow ratios could be exceedingly dangerous—these will be companies with large depreciation and other non-cash charges which could well imply higher than average price/earnings ratios. Hence these will be the very companies that other investors are avoiding.

In the world of fund management this type of problem for stock selectors has become particularly acute with the advent of mega-funds such as the Fidelity Magellan fund. Funds such as Magellan are so huge that even 'large' investments of, say, \$1 billion, amount to only a small percentage (less than 2%) of the fund's total size. Hence even apparently huge investments have a limited effect on portfolio performance. And further, the fact is that although a \$1 billion investment may only represent a relatively small proportion of the fund, it could be a declarable stake in the company acquired! The effect is to push the big mutual funds towards very large capitalisation issues, in the US into companies like Microsoft or General Electric. But the effect of this is that, in the race for relative performance, the mega-fund managers are effectively reduced to a game of outguessing their major competitors on the relative valuation merits of the fifty or so largest capitalisation stocks in the world.

This game of trying to outguess the competition can have

dramatically volatile effects on whole markets, not just on individual stock selection, and indeed can ultimately threaten global financial security. Yasuo Hamanaka was for the decade until June 1996 the senior copper trader at Sumitomo Corporation, itself a leading world player in the copper market with over 10% global market share. With credit lines of over $3bn, he dominated trading in the London Metal Exchange. Such was his grip on the market that he was affectionately known as 'Mr Copper'. His basic strategy was to place his bets in the futures market that the price would rise beyond a certain level. Then he used his buying power to leave the physical copper market short of stock and hence to raise the copper price to where he wanted it, building up huge stocks of copper for Sumitomo throughout the world as a result.

But just as Macbeth's 'overvaulting ambition' was the eventual cause of his downfall, so too did tragic fate hit Mr Copper. Late in 1995 the story began to turn. Big hedge funds (for those of you unfamiliar with the concept of hedge funds see Box 3.3) such as George Soros' Quantum Fund and Julian Robertson's Tiger Fund began to take Hamanaka on, selling copper short on the expectation of a price fall. Who would win a veritable Battle of the Titans, Hamanaka or the Hedge Funds? A classic example of a market being held at an artificial price and strategic interaction between market participants was at play. Apparently Soros gave up in March 1996, convinced that Hamanaka would do whatever was necessary to hold the price up.

Box 3.3 A Primer on Hedge Funds

'Hedge funds' are not just funds with a particular objective of 'hedging' (insuring against) particular risks such as a market downturn. In practice the name is hybrid for a wide variety of funds that attempt to deliver super normal returns by gearing up their equity to increase their resources and then investing in financial instruments some of which are not to be found in conventional investment funds. Because of some well-publicised scandals, hedge funds are sometimes viewed as the 'Wild West' of the financial services industry but this is unfair. The extent of the final risk assumed in each fund varies enormously between the different funds, from funds that assume small gearing and take relatively safe hedged bets, to others that take on huge leverage and engage in all kinds of wild gambles.

As an example of one additional technique used by hedge-fund managers to attempt to increase investor returns, consider the practice of 'selling short'. A conventional fund manager invests in securities and markets that he feels to be undervalued. A hedge-fund manager will argue that such a practice is only half the story and he will try to increase returns by identifying and profiting from securities that are overvalued just as much as from those that are undervalued. One method to achieve this is as follows. Having identified an overvalued stock through his own research, the hedge-fund manager borrows the share from a long-term holder of the stock, or a bank specialised in stock lending. Having borrowed it, the hedge fund manager then sells the stock on the market, investing the money raised in cash or in other securities. If his hunch is right and the security which he has sold short is overvalued, a subsequent correction in price will ensure that he can re-buy the stock on the market at a later date using a proportion of the funds he has already raised in the initial transaction, pay back the stock lender his shares, and pocket the remaining money as profit.

As far as the set of financial instruments a hedge-fund manager will consider, anything is fair game. As well as ordinary shares, a hedge fund will invest in a wider range of derivative instruments including futures and options that we first met in 'Arrow's World' of Chapter 1. A full description of such instruments would require a book in itself but the reader can gain an understanding of the power of such instruments by considering the following example. A 'call option' on a share gives its holder the right to buy the underlying share at a pre-specified price (the 'exercise price') up to some specified future date. Imagine the underlying share is trading at $50 a share and the exercise price on the option is $60. The option has hence no 'intrinsic value' (no one would exercise the option to buy at $60 when the same share could be bought at $50 in the market—this is sometimes referred to as the option being 'out of the money'). However, the option will have some 'time value', that reflects the fact that until the option expires, the price of the share might rise above $60 in the market and hence the option would gain intrinsic value. This 'time value' is dependent on several factors which need not concern us but for the sake of this example, let us say that the time value is 5 cents. Imagine now the stock rises 30% in the market (to $65 per share) on the back of a better profits outlook. The option now is 'in the money' and its price will rise to around $5.05 ($5 intrinsic value and 5 cents time value).

In the above example, a conventional fund manager would have enjoyed a 30% return on a $50 investment; the hedge-fund manager, who invested in the option, would enjoy over a hundred-fold return on a 5 cent investment!

Readers will no doubt be familiar with some of the global hedge funds of fame such as Soros' Quantum Fund or Robertsons' Tiger Fund and also with some of the rather infamous ones such as Long Term Capital Management discussed later in this chapter. Less well known but of increasing importance in capital markets is a veritable 'cottage industry' of hedge funds set up by talented fund managers perhaps tired of managing institutional funds on a very restricted basis. Smaller but extremely successful aggressive hedge funds in the UK include Egerton Capital run by Morgan Grenfell's former star European fund manager John Armitage, and the Sloan Robinson Investment Fund built up by a set of former skilful fund managers from the fund management group LGT.

But others refused to give in. Rumours circulated that Hamanaka's trading tactics had finally persuaded Sumitomo to remove him from the job. Wily market speculators such as Herbert Black from American Iron and Metals kept selling short, reputedly becoming a complete insomniac as the battle with Hamanaka warmed up. Black was convinced that when a workers' strike at a large mine of Chilean copper giant Codelco was averted in May and warehouse inventories failed to drop, this was a key signal that true fundamental supply was not scarce and the price of copper would head lower. On June 6th, the bubble finally burst and the copper price fell 15% in a day, with more to come over the following week. Some estimates put Sumitomo's losses as high as $4bn as a result of the market collapse. Black is reputed to have netted a tidy $50m, more than enough to compensate for a few nights' lost sleep and certainly enough to have allowed him to add to his reputed $10m collection of English Chippendale furniture.

This example of high-stakes poker is not a once in a life-time experience in financial markets and is repeated continually, not just between private sector participants but also in games between the private and public sectors in currency markets, for example. A clear example was the crisis within the Exchange Rate Mechanism (ERM) of the European Monetary System in September 1992. In this case, players in the currency markets took large short positions against the lira, sterling and the peseta for various reasons. Firstly, the currency operators noticed that inflation rates in Italy, Spain and Britain had failed to converge to German rates, leading to accumulated real appreciation of these currencies against the deutschmark. For example, although the inflation rate in Italy over the 1988–1992 period was in the range 5–6% per annum, this was substantially more than the rate in Germany, leading to a cumulative real appreciation of the lira against the deutschmark of nearly 20%. Secondly, European countries were unsynchronised, with German unification and the boom that entailed putting upward pressure on German interest rates at a time when recession or high employment was threatening to bite elsewhere in Europe. Finally, there was political evidence emerging of popular resistance to Maastricht, most notably in a Danish referendum where Viking independence asserted itself and the 'no' votes came out on top.

The net result was that the relevant governments and the private sector speculators took fundamentally different views on the fair value of the lira, the peseta and sterling, the former selling reserves to prop up the local currency; the latter selling the domestic currency short. In a strategic battle amounting to 'bluff', with governments using reserves to try to reverse the tide against their currencies, the eventual result was a market crash, as both the lira and sterling were forced out of the ERM and the peseta was devalued. Soros this time was a reputed billion dollar winner, a sufficient war chest to prepare for the copper market bubble we already discussed!

The Sumitomo scandal of 1995 or the earlier ERM debacle of 1992 are not just isolated incidents of strategic interaction between market participants. Such games are played out daily on the world's capital markets, and notice that we are not just talking about emerging markets but about strategic games at the heart of the developed world's capital markets. If we confine ourselves to currency markets alone, then since 1975 there have been almost ninety crashes, an average of over three per year. What do these examples teach us? Again the message is that passive portfolio indexing is nothing more than the decision to be driven by the winds of fickle fortune rather than the cool air of dispassionate deduction. While in the deductive world of CAPM, portfolio indexing emerges as a winning strategy, we simply do not live in that world and there can be no presumption in a strategic world that portfolio indexing is the best strategy for an investor to follow (for a break now go to Box 3.4 to really get your mind thinking about rationality in a strategic framework).

Box 3.4 The Newcomb Paradox—Outguessing your Guardian Angel

Just to leave you as sleepless as Herbert Black in the game of outguessing your opponent, consider the following paradox invented by Professor William Newcomb. An extra-terrestrial being in whom you have nearly complete confidence to predict your actions (say 99% confidence) is going to predict what you will do in the following situation. There are two boxes sitting on a table, one opaque, the other clear. The clear box contains $1000. The opaque box contains either $1m or $0. You have the choice between two actions; either taking what is in both boxes or taking whatever is in the opaque box only. The twist is this. If the being predicts you will take both boxes, he will put nothing in the opaque box. If, however, he predicts you will take only the opaque box, he will put the $1m in that box. First the being makes his prediction, second he puts the $1m in the box or not, depending on his prediction, thirdly you choose. What should you do?

Again there are competing views on what is rational to do. One argument (sometimes referred to as the 'dominance' argument) suggests you take both boxes. Why? If the being has put the money in the box, then by taking both boxes you get the $1m and $1000 (which is better than just $1m if you just take the opaque box), while if the being has not put the $1m in the box, again by taking both boxes you get something ($1000) as opposed to nothing.

Looks like a watertight argument. But now consider this. In terms of maximising expected utility there is a strong argument for just taking the opaque box. The expected value of this action is a high number (0.99 × $1m). However, the expected value of taking both boxes is much lower (0.99 × $1000) + (0.01 × $1m). Which principle of rationality would you follow? When you have decided, change the numbers of the payoffs and see if this changes your view. For example, if you believe in the dominance argument, now assume that there is only one cent in the clear box and either $10m or nothing in the opaque box. Are you still so sure that taking both boxes is best? The quest for the holy grail of rationality can drive you mad!

TIME AND ITS INTRICACIES

When we permit time to enter the decision-making process explicitly, we potentially introduce even greater complexity into strategic decision making. Regarding the interaction between investors, richer strategies can now be devised (see Box 3.5 for an introduction), for now the shrewd investor need not reveal his cards all at once but can devise 'wait-and-see' and other strategies designed to ensure better performance within a medium-term time framework. What follows will give the investor an insight into two of the important issues regarding decision making over time. These insights bring to the fore a problem with the rather straightforward concept of instrumental rationality assumed in CAPM. We can remember from Chapter 1 that instrumental rationality is identified with the ability of an individual to choose actions which best satisfy that individual's objectives. With our discussions on imperfect information and strategy, we can already see that, even if one accepts such a view of rationality, it can be very hard to pinpoint what the instrumentally rational thing to do is in some cases. And now for something even more complex! The first insight relates to the nature of the profit generation process; the second relates to the use of money as an asset which is particularly important when we consider time explicitly. Each issue is examined separately below.

Box 3.5 Strategy—on Odysseus, Girls and Mafiosi

One of the most famous stories to illustrate some of the issues raised for strategic decision making when individuals have the capacity to make decisions over time comes from Classical literature. The Greek hero Odysseus, after successfully participating in the rescue of Helen of Troy, experiences many adventures on an eventful trip home, including visits to drug-addicts, giants, sorcerers, and the like, not to mention various ship-wrecks and being held against his will for seven years while Calypso tries to persuade him to marry her! Poor guy!

One interesting anecdote amidst all these adventures is when his boat has to sail past two Sirens living on a little island in the Straits of Messina between Sicily and the Italian coast. In Greek myth the Sirens were beautiful female creatures with the power to draw men to destruction through their melodies. Male readers beware—there are still some of them around!

Odysseus faces a problem with which some of us will be familiar—he would like to hear the music without having to face the music! In order to escape being lured to the rocks on the island where certain death awaits him and his crew, Odysseus fills the ears of his sailors with wax but leaves his own unblocked. He then instructs his sailors to tie him up to the ship's mast. He instructs them to ignore his gesticulations to be unbound until the ship is well past the island. Thus he was able to enjoy the Sirens' song without falling into their trap. Hence this strategy seemed like short-term madness, but was long-term successful. According to the myth, the Sirens are so annoyed by Odysseus' escape that they subsequently drown themselves.

Readers may be interested to know that even Odysseus did not always get things his own way, whatever his cunning, although he was definitely a dangerous man to have as an enemy. In an attempt to avoid going to the Trojan war in the first place, he had tried to feign insanity as a reason not to be sent to fight. Alas the ruse was exposed to the army by Palamedes, a Greek genius credited incidentally with inventing the game of draughts. Odysseus was not amused. In revenge, he forged a letter purportedly from enemy HQ, arranging for Palamedes to betray the Greeks in return for a handsome payoff in terms of gold. Odysseus then hid some gold in Palamedes' tent and conveniently let the forged letter slip into the hands of the army. The latter then marched straight into Palamedes' tent, found the gold, and stoned him to death. The implicit strategic lesson has been taken on board by Mafiosi and cartels around the world ever since—don't get even, get revenge!

Notice an important point of the tale. Odysseus was not fully rational in the sense of Chapter 1, for a fully rational person would not have had to resort to the method chosen by Odysseus to avoid the Sirens. But the point is that the lack of full rationality did not prevent Odysseus from achieving the same goal as a fully rational person. Imperfection in rationality does not necessarily imply imperfection in achievement. What was important here was that Odysseus was aware of his limitations and acted to circumvent them. The practical implications of this are many-fold, not just in finance. An interesting case is the Norwegian 'Law of Psychic Health Protection' where people may seek irrevocable admission to a mental hospital, despite the possibility of later wishing to revoke that request. In fact a psychiatrist may lay down a condition for admission that the patient stays for several weeks, whatever the patient subsequently requests.

The Profit Generation Process in Oligopolies

The issue here is that, within a dynamic environment, the whole nature of the profit generation process itself becomes subject to strategic intrigue between companies, adding a further layer of expectations complexity to the investor's decision problem. To come to grips with some of the problems involved, consider the issue of a cartel. A cartel is simply a group of independent producers who connive to behave collectively as a monopoly. Each member of the cartel agrees to produce less than he otherwise would under unrestricted competition with the overall objective of driving up the industry price to the benefit of all the cartel members. The effect can be dramatic, as oil experts will immediately remember various cartel moves within OPEC which had the effect of driving prices from under $2 a barrel in the early 1970s to over $34 a barrel a decade later.

But all cartels have an Achilles' heel—however desirable the arrangement is to the group as a whole, for any single member it pays to 'cheat' on the deal. The cheat enjoys the higher prices generated by the cartel, in addition to the higher output secretly engineered by himself. Of course, if all cheat, the cartel collapses. Typically we could summarise the potential payoffs of a simple 'duopoly' (two producers in the market) cartel as in Table 3.1 below, which illustrates clearly the tension between collusion and competition, or honesty and lies.

Table 3.1 Hypothetical Profits ($m) in a Market Duopoly

		COMPANY A	
		COLLUDE	CHEAT
COMPANY B	COLLUDE	(4, 4)	(5, 1)
	CHEAT	(1, 5)	(2, 2)

Each bracket contains the payoff of the two firms (with company A's profits first under different assumptions about whether the two firms collude or not. When both companies 'cheat' on the cartel agreement by increasing output, overall industry output will be high and prices low, leaving each firm with a small profit. When both companies keep the cartel agreement and reduce their individual output, industry output will be low and prices high. However, each firm does best of all when it alone cheats–the other firm's low output helps keep industry output down and prices up, while the turncoat firm benefits by selling a higher output at this price.

What is likely to happen, given this structure of payoffs if the two participants interact with each other year in and year out in the market? It is not difficult to see that the market could easily go through periods of collusion and no-collusion. Perhaps precommitments or a secret deal by each firm can initially sustain the cartel; then the danger is that one firm exercises the short-term incentive to cheat, which when discovered could easily lead to 'punishment' by the cheated cartel member (or members in a more general setting). Punishment may have the desired effect of bringing the renegade cartel member to heel and collusion can be re-established. One can get a feel for the issues by referring back to the earlier discussion of OPEC. When prices were held up in the 1980s, principally by the dramatic cutbacks in production of over 50% in Saudi Arabia, other countries slowly but surely started to cheat on their output quotas. Eventually Saudi Arabia disciplined the market, driving prices down to below $10 a barrel by 1986 (see Figure 3.1).

The fundamental point of the above analysis for portfolio management is that production decisions by companies

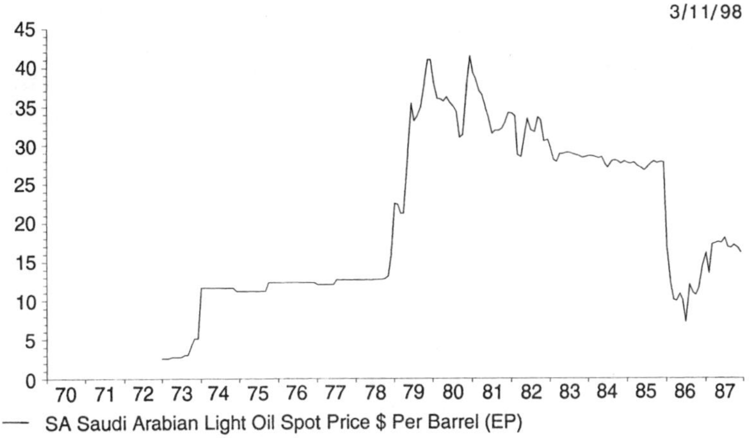

Figure 3.1 The Rise and Fall of the Oil Cartel 1970–1987

Source: Reproduced by permission of Datastream International.

have a strategic element which can have a dramatic impact on profits. The investor in a particular company or sector needs to be aware of and form expectations about the expectations of producers and the product market outcome of those expectations, every bit as much as forming expectations about the behaviour of other investors. With such an intricate web of expectations, the evolution of stock market valuations can clearly be extremely volatile and the notion of a CAPM-type equilibrium starts to look even more far-fetched. So too does its recommendation of portfolio indexing. In times of great uncertainties in the oil market, does it necessarily make sense to hold large capitalisation oil stocks just because they are large parts of some stock market indices?

The Value of Money in a Dynamic Environment

The issue here is how money, interest rates and liquidity are intertwined with the portfolio investment process. In CAPM, money is simply seen as the incarnation of an individual's desire to avoid market risk, as everything he does not hold in the market portfolio is simply held in cash. In CAPM there is a dichotomy between the 'known' (the interest rate on cash) and the 'unknown' (the return over a particular period on other assets—though of course the unknown is, according to CAPM, reducible to statistics).

But money serves another function which CAPM fails to capture, that is money is the perfect asset to hold if one wants to adopt a 'wait-and-see' strategy within the sort of uncertain world described in this chapter where markets may be stretched from fair valuations because of information asymmetries and strategic issues—holding cash gives the individual investor time to think. To hold a large cash balance is not necessarily a sign of a particularly risk-averse investor; it can equally well be the strategy of an investor who is playing for time, waiting for the right moment to enter the market. Cash is a war chest every bit as much as a safe haven.

Why is cash the best strategic instrument for the 'wait-and-see' policy rather than any other financial asset traded on a regular market? After all, surely stocks or bonds could equally well be held over the waiting period and then sold at the appropriate moment. The answer is that to use any other asset runs the risk that, at the moment you want to sell, this particular asset is going through a 'bear' market phase with prices artificially depressed. In such a case, any forced sale will involve an unnecessary capital loss. Only an investment in cash, or near cash, does not entail this risk (and then only so long as there is no hyper inflation!). This is ultimately what is meant by the liquidity advantage of money.

HYSTERESIS EFFECTS AND THE LIMITS OF ARBITRAGE

An implicit underlying theme in all of the sections of this chapter has been the failure of arbitrage to ensure quick and smooth self-adjustment of markets to tensions and shocks. Whether it be because of imperfect information or strategic intrigue we have seen reasons for stocks and markets to stray from equilibrium values for protracted periods of time and then to exhibit violent changes. In fact it is worth focusing on the concept of arbitrage and its limits as we bring the various themes of the chapter together. CAPM assumes that the financial system is self-adjusting or homeostatic, in the sense that shocks that move equity and bond markets away from equilibrium quickly lead to counterbalancing forces which will return the market to its initial equilibrium when the shock abates. This ensures that individual shares remain on the securities market line and that there is a stable relation between stock market returns and interest rates (the risk premium—readers might like to refresh their memories of this by turning back to Figures 2.6

and 2.7 in Chapter 2). Although it is never explicitly stated in the CAPM analysis, it is implicitly assumed that there are a set of arbitrageurs who will iron out any price discrepancies (in individual stocks and between equity and fixed income markets) to ensure a perpetual situation of equilibrium or at least near-equilibrium.

However, what we have seen in the previous sections of this chapter is that in reality, because of strategic intrigue and imperfect information flows, stocks and markets appear at times to be driven to far-from-equilibrium positions. Obviously, in the world as we have been describing it, arbitrage works imperfectly. A little thought will reveal why.

In pure theory, an arbitrageur smoothes out price differences between identical goods (so called 'perfect' substitutes), earning the differential between the prices as a reward for his endeavour (see for example the Modigliani–Miller argument in Chapter 1). If the price of a security falls below that of a dearer perfect substitute, the arbitrageur sells 'short' the relatively high priced security and invests in the relatively low priced one and vice versa. The arbitrage process continues until prices are equilibrated. In a CAPM world, the argument is that it should usually be easy to find a security with similar risk and hence return characteristics to an under-or-over priced counterpart so long as the overall market contains a sufficient number of securities ensuring that arbitrage between individual securities works.

But what if the world is as we have described it in this chapter? Risk characteristics of individual securities may well now not be able to be captured by simple statistical parameters. The unquantifiable uncertainty prevents the arbitrageur from doing his work as he cannot find counterpart securities to perform his work—it takes two to tango in the arbitrageur's world! Hence stocks can easily stray from the securities market line and remain over or undervalued for considerable periods of time.

Arbitrage between markets (such as the bond and equity

markets) is even more problematical in the world as we have described it. Even if we ignore the previous paragraph and make the bold assumption that arbitrage can help gravitate the relative prices of individual securities towards their fair values, it does not help to pin down the overall price of stocks or bonds as a whole. This is another way of saying that we should expect the market risk premium to be a difficult concept to catch, like chasing one's shadow, which is exactly the case in the actual financial world. Risk premia of equities over bonds, even in developed markets, can appear stable but then gyrate wildly in times of uncertainty. An arbitrageur who believes, for example, that stocks as a whole are undervalued relative to bonds has no riskless way to perform his arbitrage work. Obviously he can buy stocks and sell bonds short as a portfolio strategy but this is now a long way from arbitrage as he is exposed to investment risk, not just from the fact that his view on long-term relative valuation between these different asset classes may be wrong, but also that even if he is right his short-term timing may be wrong. Inevitably arbitrage activity between asset classes will be limited for these reasons, which again implies markets can stray from equilibrium for drawn-out periods, unlike the CAPM analysis with its perpetual static equilibrium.

The behaviour of Japanese equities over the 1980s illustrates clearly the limits of arbitrage even in major financial markets (Figure 3.2). Over the period, equities climbed to a peak valuation of over 60 × earnings, levels inconsistent with dividend and earnings growth. Why did arbitrage fail to halt the climb over so long a period? The reason was that the arbitrageur faced two types of uncertainty: investment uncertainty (what was the fair value of the market in the absence of a perfect substitute to measure it against); and timing uncertainty (for how long could prices stay out of line in the absence of a perfect arbitrage opportunity). Any investor who sold Japanese stocks short in 1985 when the P/E ratio reached an already stretched 30 × would have

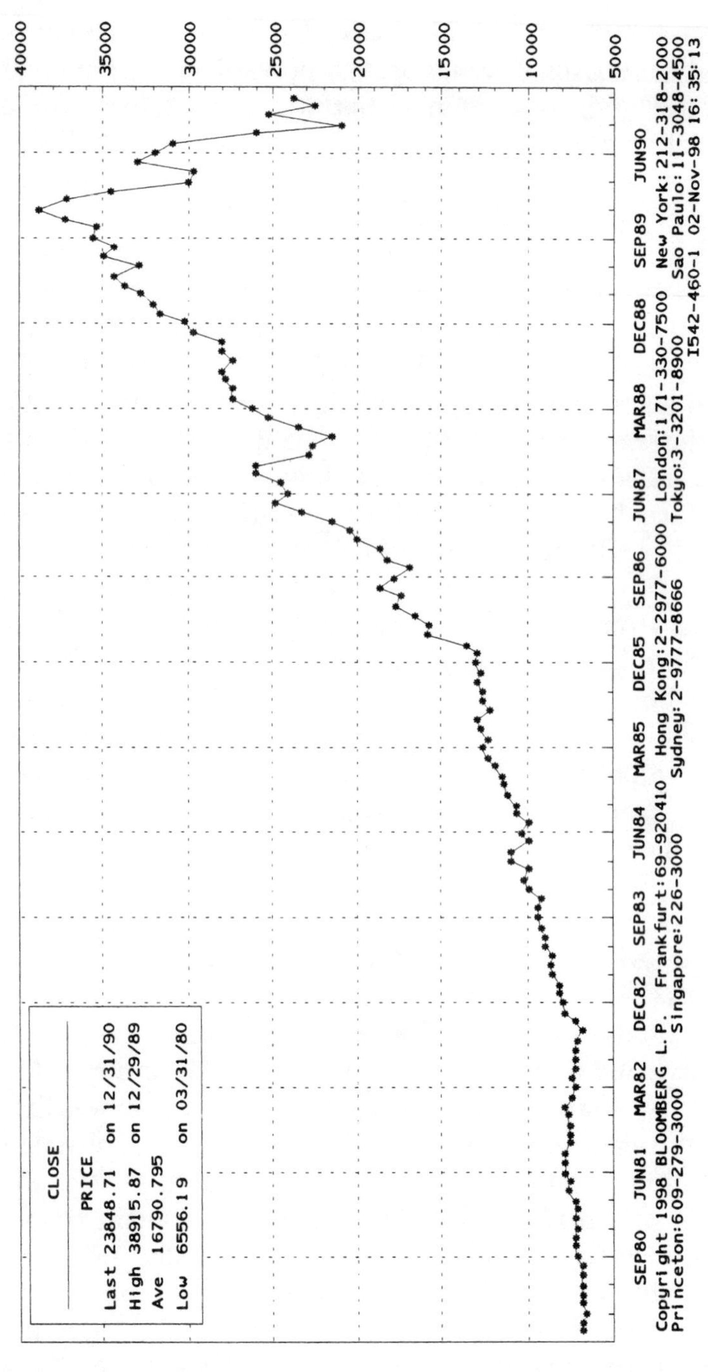

Figure 3.2 Japanese Equity Market 1980–1990

Source: Bloomberg

lost his shirt, with the multiple climbing to 60 × just over a year later on the back of a major bull run.

Another example of the failure of arbitrage that will surely go down in the history books is the failure associated with the downturn of equity markets in the second half of 1998 and the near collapse of one of the global leading hedge funds, Long Term Capital International (LTCM). Originally set up by the ebullient ex-Salomon Bros Vice-Chairman John Meriwether, and employing some of the rocket scientists of the academic part of the financial community, including Nobel prize winners Robert Merton and Myron Scholes, LTCM was a highly leveraged fund with assets at its peak of nearly $100bn supported on a capital base of under $5bn). The fund specialised in arbitrage.

Most of the fund's exposure was in the developed markets of the world, the US, Europe and Japan, rather than in the emerging markets of the Asia or Latin America. One basic strategy of the fund was to engage in 'credit spreads'. This was the strategy of speculating on the improvement or deterioration in the credit rating and hence the yield of particular bonds (the fund would go long of bonds thought to be likely to improve in quality and short of those thought likely to be enjoying too glamorous a rating). Simultaneously, the fund would take 'balancing' positions in appropriate core bonds to hedge market risk. To the unwary eye, this might seem like riskless arbitrage.

For a while the trick worked. For example, the fund reputedly made multimillion dollar gains by correctly anticipating a narrowing of spreads of different sovereign issues within the European bond market, as Europe prepared for European Monetary Union. Figure 3.3 below shows that yields on Spanish government bonds, for example, did indeed narrow sharply in the run up to EMU, as did the spread on Italian, Portuguese and Greek issues, giving the possibility for LTCM to profit from long-positions in South European official debt hedged by a short on deutschmark government issues.

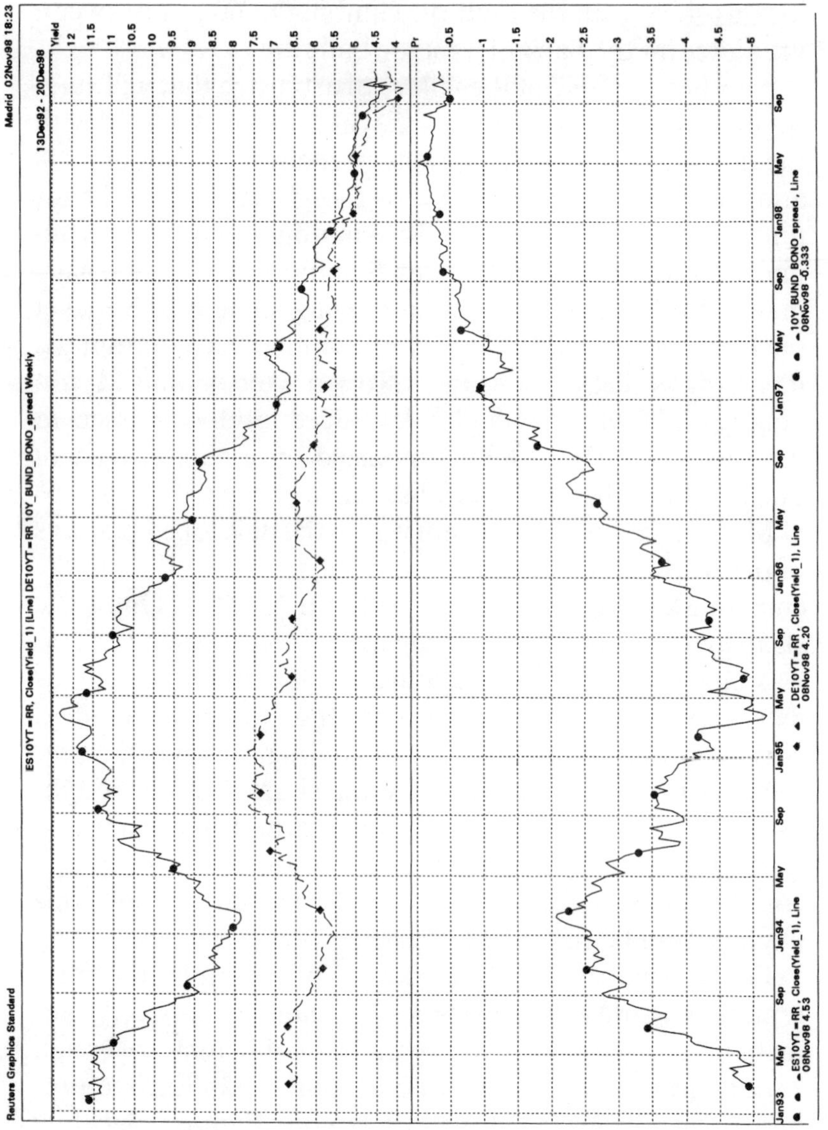

Figure 3.3 Peseta versus Deutschmark Yield Spread Jan. 1997–June 1998 *Source*: Reproduced by permission of Reuters Ltd.

However, when Russia defaulted on its international obligations in August 1998, a contagion effect in bond markets caused a flight to quality and credit spreads in bond markets suddenly widened, including those in Greece where the fund was exposed. These effects were exacerbated by the high degree of leverage the fund had assumed at nearly twenty times its capital base. Margin calls on its futures positions drained liquidity and the fund was faced with the prospect of having to unwind positions to meet these cash calls. Unfortunately unwinding these positions threatened to move the markets further against the underlying bet, creating a potentially vicious circle. In the end, the situation was so serious that the Federal Reserve encouraged fifteen of the US leading investment banks to put up a multi-billion dollar rescue package to avoid a debacle.

With imperfect arbitrage, financial markets, rather than being self-correcting when disturbed from equilibrium, instead exhibit what is referred to as hysteresis effects. In the financial market context, hysteresis implies that when a shock is applied to some variable and then removed, the variable does not necessarily spring back to the original *status quo* valuation (for more on the general applicability of hysteresis see Box 3.6). Such a phenomenon has two important implications for our analysis of financial markets. Firstly, financial shocks can linger in their effects for years, and secondly, financial surprises can permanently change the basis of valuation of securities.

The simplest way to see this is what happens if a bank run gathers momentum. Banks epitomise the combination of high leverage that we see in hedge funds together with a mismatch betwen relatively illiquid assets (loans) but liquid liabilities (deposits). While optimism is high, depositors are happy to leave an increasing amount of cash deposited at the bank. The bank, in turn, is happy to lend and may go down the quality curve in search of the necessary borrowers, sacrificing normally required collateral rules in order to meet lending targets—especially so if moral hazard is at

Box 3.6 The History of Hysteresis

Hysteresis as a phenomenon was first coined by the Dundonian physicist James Alfred Ewing. Ewing achieved international fame for being in charge of the Room 40 decipher group during the First World War—this was the team that deciphered the telegram from the then German foreign secretary Dr Zimmerman, suggesting an alliance of Mexico with Germany and Japan, which, if successful, would have placed Texas, New Mexico and Arizona in Mexican hands! In essence the distinguishing feature of a system or of a variable in the system cannot be explained without reference to the past history of the system or variable itself.

For example, from our early days in physics classes we can remember that the magnetisation of a ferric metal permanently changes the electromagnetic characteristics of the metal—it does not return to its initial electromagnetic state when the magnetising force is removed. There are a host of examples of this type of phenomenon in economics. One interesting example is the work of Professor Rod Cross on unemployment. Rather than there being a 'natural rate' of unemployment about which the economy oscillates, Cross argues convincingly that shocks to output can have permanent effects on potential output—for example a prolonged recession engineered by monetary tightening to reduce inflation may increase the stock of long-term unemployed and the stock of scrap real capital. When monetary conditions are subsequently eased, it is not correct to assume that these workers and this machinery can be brought back to work as if nothing had happened. The former have lost motivation and skills; the latter may be technologically obsolete. In other words, hysteresis is at work.

work! However, if a sudden shock or rumour entails that depositors lose confidence and withdraw funds *en masse*, the bank can be quickly forced into liquidation and even insolvency if capital resources are insufficient. Inevitably the share price of the bank in question plummets, and there is no invisible hand to guide valuations back to initial levels once the panic subsides—long-term or even permanent damage to the relevant share price is the inevitable result.

Notice yet again the crucial and in the above case tragic participation of financial agents in the final result—depositors through their actions precipitate the very event they have most to fear. George Soros refers to this phenomenon as the 'participating function'—in far from equilibrium situations, investors are not mere automatons computing optimal portfolios as in CAPM, but rather they specifically participate in the evolution of events themselves.

Hysteresis effects are not just relevant in credit markets but can abound in equity markets as well. To see the effects of hysteresis in such a context, we need look no further than the US stock market to see that not all crashes lead to quick or complete recoveries. The Wall Street reverses of 1893 and 1929 had rather different dynamics than the 1987 crash. In both the 1893 and 1929 crashes, the financial effects were transmitted to the real economy principally via a seriously damaged banking system that then made it difficult to reflate when demand collapsed. This led to genuine bear markets. In 1893 the market tumble, initially driven by fears of an abandonment of dollar/gold convertibility, led to a wave of insolvencies of companies and banks, with the panic so great that in August there was a nationwide suspension of the convertibility of bank deposits into cash. The economy took four years to recover and real share price valuations did not return to pre-crash values for a decade.

The Wall Street crash of 1929 was even more dramatic, coming as it did after an 8 years' bull run in equities that had driven valuations over 300% higher. Ironically however, over this period there was a substantial inconsistency in US monetary policy that was ultimately unsustainable. That inconsistency was the Federal Reserve being simultaneously committed to a 'lender of last resort' function, while at the same time being committed to maintaining the 'gold standard'—that is the commitment to swap dollars into gold and *vice versa* at a fixed price. In line with the discussion we have already had on the problems of moral hazard for the banking system, the 1920s saw a mushrooming of credit in the US with banks undertaking riskier projects that they might have done without the 'lender of last resort' safety net. As banks increased their lending they brought nearer the day when the Fed might be called upon to inject liquidity into the banking system to such a degree as to jeopardise its ability to maintain its promise to exchange currency for gold at a fixed price. Before doomsday, the stock market crashed and again the financial crash had real economic effects, exacerbated by widespread banking collapses (as the Fed jettisoned the lender of last resort role to maintain its commitment to the gold standard, at least until 1933) and a huge contraction of the money supply led to the shutdown and mothballing of real capacity in the economy. The depression in this case lasted a decade and shares did not recover for a staggering twenty five years (see Figure 3.4).

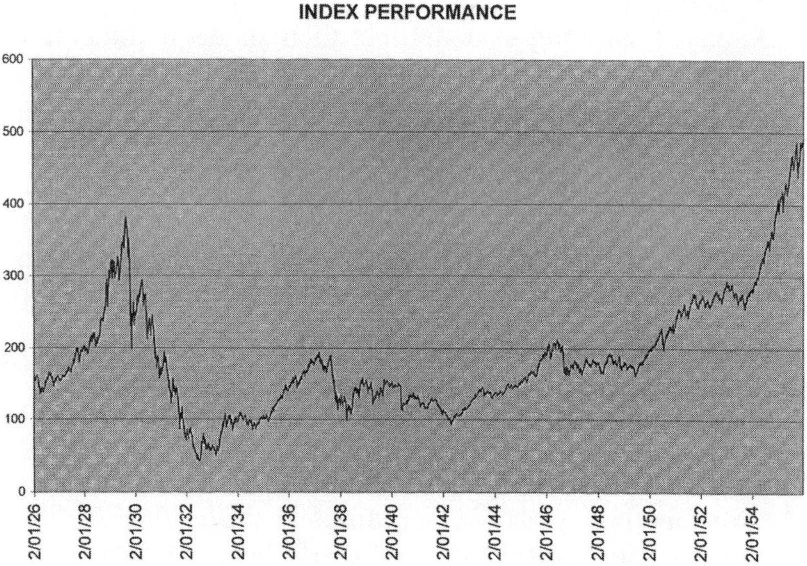

Figure 3.4 The 1929 Wall Street Crash and its Lingering Effects

Source: Dow Jones Indexes, with permission.

CONCLUSIONS

At this point it is worthwhile to draw some provisional conclusions. CAPM is an uncomfortable combination of exact formulas but highly specialised assumptions which has been used to establish a case for portfolio indexing as the best combination of risk and return available to the investor. However, if we are serious about understanding the uncertain nature of securities markets and how they operate, the foundations of the CAPM approach need to be abandoned.

Both market failure and government failure are pervasive in modern financial systems. Information is distributed unevenly and incompletely in markets and government-led interventions can make things worse rather than better via issues such as moral hazard. Further, investors in general are not vested with full statistical information about the investment opportunities open to them simply because the uncertainties surrounding prospective investment returns cannot be well captured by statistical concepts. Furthermore, the nature of interaction between market participants forces humans to act strategically, introducing further uncertainties into the investment process. Investors are landed in a world of subjective beliefs about the beliefs of other investors and producers, and subjective beliefs about subjective beliefs. In forming these beliefs market participants can affect the returns on the very investments they are contemplating. Finally, as investors struggle to interpret the environment in which they have to invest, they may adopt wait-and-see strategies designed to buy time—again in so doing they may affect the very environment they are trying to comprehend. All the above features of markets can lead stocks, individual markets and ultimately global markets into boom/bust cycles with shares wandering far from equilibrium values as implied by a model such as CAPM, with arbitrageurs unable or unwilling to commit the necessary capital to maintain equilibrium.

With the abandonment of the CAPM paradigm goes with it the desertion of one of its central implications, that of market indexing. The passive asset allocation strategy as an optimal portfolio response to uncertainty simply loses relevance in the world that we have been describing. Investors now cannot rely on market prices conveying the proper information about security or market potential returns or depend on the market to self-select the optimal risk/return portfolio. In the complex world of securities markets, indexing is little more than the decision to follow the crowd while the crowd itself looks around helplessly for guidance on what to do.

Amid the uncertainty, financial markets will be volatile as investors with differing information and views of the odds, as well as different objectives and time scales, digest every new piece of information or misinformation for clues to the true underlying prospective returns. If you like, the automatic pilot is being fed unreliable signals and cannot be trusted to guide us to the chosen destination. The only solution is renewed manual control. Just how this manual control might work is the theme of the next chapter.

4

An Alternative—Financial Market Strategy in the Twilight

COMPLEX WORLDS

The financial world can be thought of as an extremely complicated and at times ill-defined system with information unevenly distributed amongst market participants and in which agents' expectations impinge on current outcomes but where the actual history of outcomes affects those agents' very expectations. There can be no presumption of a unique deductively rational solution for the values and time paths of financial variables such as stock prices in such a system. In fact, well-defined rational behaviour is elusive and chimerical in many cases in such a world, as investors are propelled into a world of induction and away from the deductive world of CAPM. In such an environment, there is ample scope for stocks and markets to be volatile, following patterns inconsistent with so-called market fundamentals (for a discussion on how the world as we have described it compares with 'Chaos Theory', see Box 4.1 below).

In this world, the notion of market fundamentals and efficient prices has little or no meaning, and there can be little presumption that passive portfolio indexing is the best

Box 4.1 Complexity versus Chaos

Readers need to be careful to distinguish the 'complex' world described in the text from another world in which volatility is evident, that is the world of 'Chaos Theory'. The latter is a somewhat misleading term but refers to the fact that it is perfectly possible for observations that look random to have an underlying and sometimes simple mathematical logic. An elementary mathematical equation to describe the movement of a variable over time may, with suitable parameters, produce startling patterns of randomness, and these patterns may be extremely sensitive to the parameters of the equation and the initial value used in the equation. For example, the equation $y_{t+1} = ky_t - ky_t^2$ (subscripts referring to time, k being a constant and y the variable) can generate extremely random looking series for certain values of k and a suitable starting point. The chart below shows how the variable will evolve for an initial value of y of 0.99 and a value for k of 3.94. But small changes to these numbers will generate completely different-looking series. The interested reader is referred to the contribution by William Baumol in Lofthouse *Readings in Investments.*

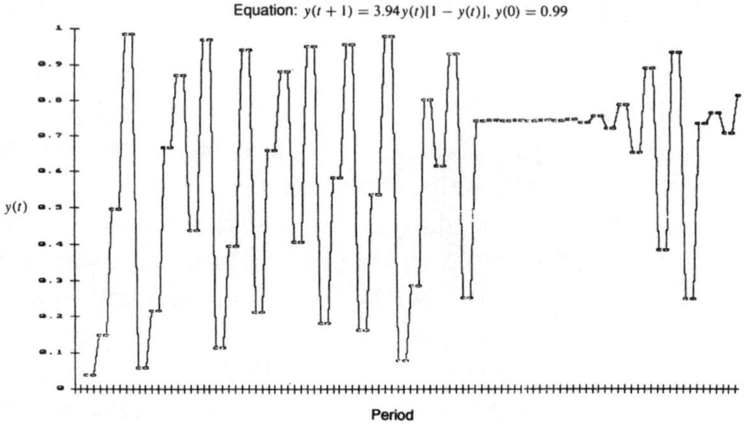

Chaotic time path

Source: Baumol, W.J. 1988. The chaos phenomenon: a nightmare for forecasters. *LSE Quarterly*, 1, March, 99–114.

This extreme sensitivity of behaviour to small changes in the process generating the data gives rise to the so-called 'butterfly-wing effect' in chaos theory, meaning that if the weather in London is determined by a chaotic process, the erratic flap of a butterfly's wing at New York's Kennedy airport can cause a storm at Heathrow! However, the defining characteristic of a 'chaotic' system is that while the process may be volatile and appear random, the system follows the underlying mathematical logic forever—nothing changes and nothing adapts. This is a far cry from a 'complex' system, which forms the background to this chapter—complex systems embrace the quirks of information limitations and strategy and such systems do change and do adapt.

an investor can do, or indeed anywhere near the best an investor can do in devising an investment strategy. The investor is genuinely confronted with investing, if not in complete darkness, then certainly in the twilight.

At this point the investor really has two options. One way out is to throw up his hands in despair and simply allow himself to be guided by the animal spirits Keynes conjured up to explain decision making in such circumstances. Astrological-type portfolio management techniques are in fact used by some investors to guide portfolio choice and in the bibliography you can find one reference for those of you who want to throw in the towel and star gaze (Astrology and Stock Market Forecasting by Louise McWhirter). Alternatively the investor might try to create strategies designed to deal with the complexities in the financial world that we have discussed. In some ways the astrological approach to investment is not that different from portfolio indexing in my view, because in the financial world as we have described it, a passive indexing strategy is simply the decision to allow your money to be driven by whim. Having rejected the indexing strategy on these grounds, we are forced to reject the astrological approach as well. The serious investor is surely better to attempt to devise an alternative approach, whatever the complexities of the endeavour.

DEALING WITH COMPLEXITY—INTRODUCTORY COMMENTS

By its nature the complex world forces investors to use a variety of simplifying hypotheses or rules of thumb which, while effective in economising in information gathering and processing, are fallible guides to action which may even at times lead to erroneous perceptions and actions. The ability of investors to learn which of their hypotheses are relatively robust to changing circumstances, and their ability to come up with new ideas as the financial world evolves will be critical to investment performance (see Box 4.2 for an introduction to the idea of complexity in a different setting).

Box 4.2 Complexity and Guessing Whether to Go Out for the Evening

The Belfast-born Stanford Professor, Brian Arthur, one of the key academic figures in relation to the issue of complexity and its relation to economic theory, is credited with an excellent example of complexity at work in an everyday setting. The so-called 'Bar Problem' runs as follows. Imagine one hundred people decide independently each Thursday whether or not to go to a bar that offers Irish music on Thursday evenings. There is no sure way to tell the numbers coming in advance, and the evening is enjoyable if things are not too crowded—specifically if fewer than sixty people are actually present. Notice that there is no 'deductive' or 'correct' expectations model to capture the features of this situation— potential attendees are propelled into a world of induction in trying to guess just how many people will actually show up. Also notice that communality of expectations will have perverse effects—if all believe few will go, all will go! But that obviously invalidates that belief which will now have to be revised. Similarly, if all believe most will go, nobody will go, again invalidating the belief.

What actually happens in such situations? Interestingly Arthur shows that in computer simulations of the problem with attendees following different plausible rules to guess the likely numbers attending next Thursday such as: the average of the previous four weeks; the same number as last week etc., the mean attendance converges on sixty. Readers might like to consider why the system has this equilibrium tendency and also likely to consider the crucial differences in the effects of expectations in the Bar Problem from the expectations effects at play in the Bank Problem analysed in Chapter 3.

Later in this chapter we shall examine some ways investors can try to keep the adaptive spirit which is at the heart of this approach. Before examining these issues, however, there is arguably one universal principle to follow in dealing with the uncertainties inherent in the financial world—that is the principle of survival. While fund mangers are continually learning from experience which of their hypotheses work better in normal market conditions, it is important not to be 'wiped out' in a financial crisis or meltdown. Such crises are only too common in stock markets as we have seen in Chapter 3. Avoiding as far as possible such disasters is the essence of the survival principle. In effect this principle tells us to start the investment management process the other way round, by identifying which stocks or markets to avoid before deciding in which assets to invest.

DEALING WITH COMPLEXITY—THE SURVIVAL PRINCIPLE

Knowing when not to invest is as big a secret to outperformance as knowing when to invest. I refer to this as the

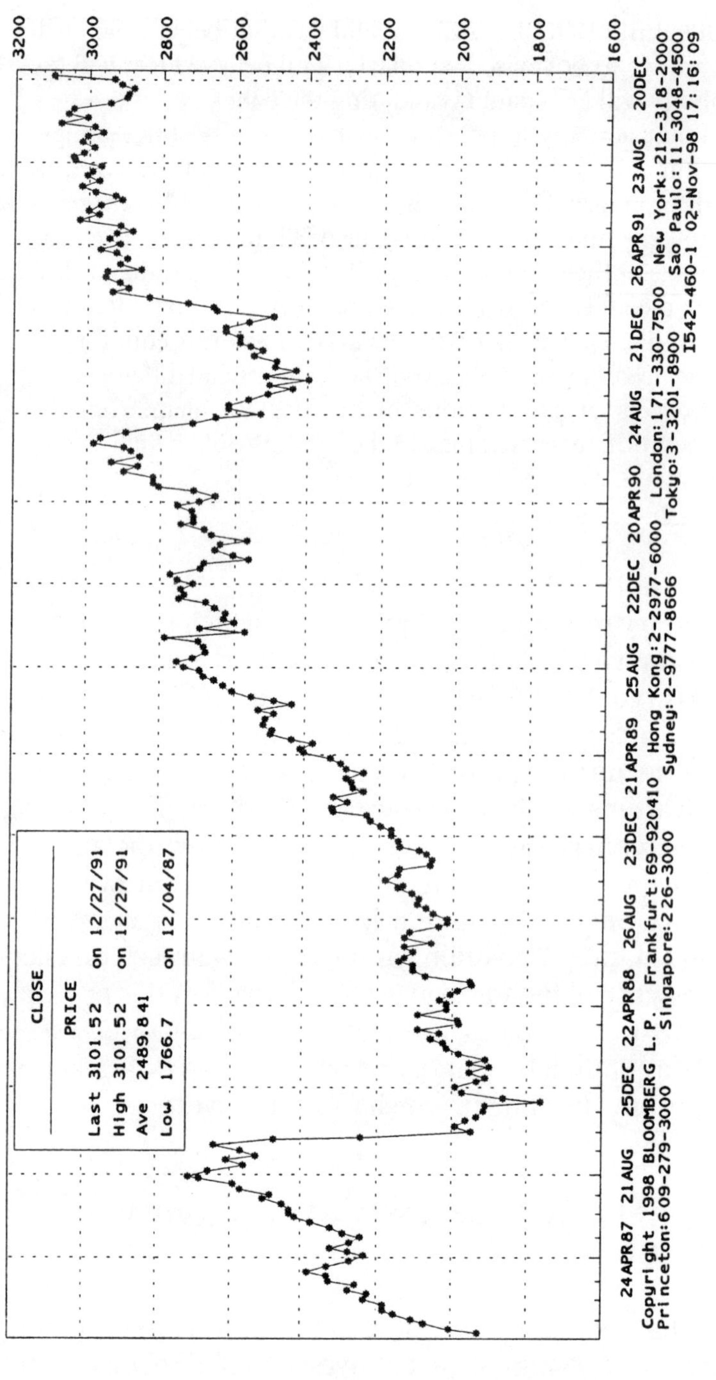

Wall Street Crash 1987

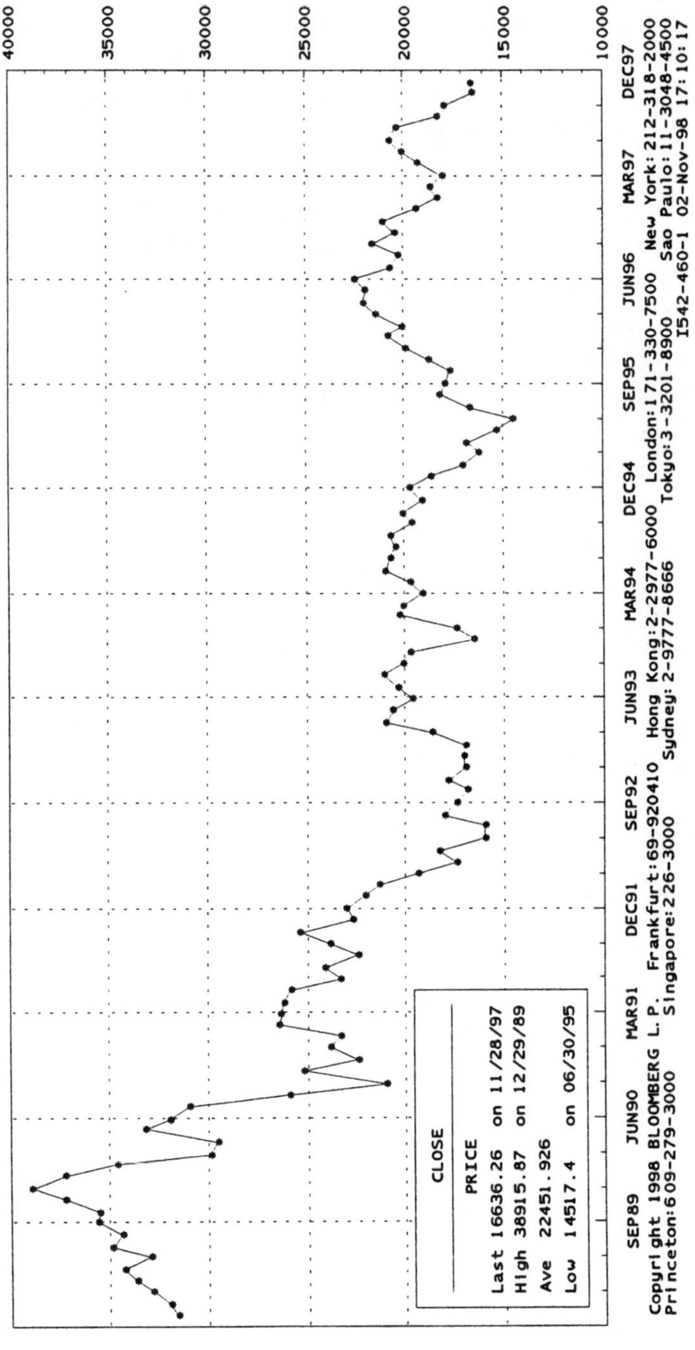

Japanese Crash 1990

Figure 4.1 Different Types of Crashes

Source: Bloomberg

survival principle of investment. The survival principle encourages us to be out of markets that are likely to suffer severe corrections. By severe corrections I have in mind a loss of over 25% in value in a short time period (say a week) or a loss of 50% or more over a longer period (such as a year). An example of the former would be the Wall Street Crash of 1987, an example of the latter would be the reversal of the Japanese stock market beginning in 1990 (see Figure 4.1). The survival principle is wholly at odds with the CAPM approach which encourages us to be fully invested across the spectrum of available stocks and markets at all times whatever the prospects. For the CAPM specialist, the survival principle is completely captured in the notion of full diversification, which aims to limit the damage rather than to avoid it.

Let us examine the survival principle further. An example from outside the financial world which may help to shed some light on the issues involved is from aviation. A Ground Proximity Warning System (GPWS) is a device designed to aid a pilot when he is flying 'blind' in uncertain terrain (through fog in mountainous terrain, for example). In such situations the captain does not have fully reliable indications of where the peaks on the mountains are relative to the plane. Both pilot and passengers are confronted with unquantifiable and potentially unpleasant uncertainty.

If the GPWS rings, any pilot immediately climbs out of the fog—a simple survival rule. Sometimes the GPWS may go off in error (the mountain was not in fact that close but the sensor detected something else), but the captain will still climb as he does not have this information. Obviously then the GPWS is not leading to 'optimal' decisions all the time, but surely it is reasonable to argue that it leads to sensible decision making under the circumstances. If you are in any doubt about this proposition, think about it next time you are landing in fog at some tiny airport in the Alps.

Another example from outside the financial world comes from mountain climbing. Towards the top of a difficult

Alpine peak, you are suddenly confronted with a rapid and dangerous change in weather conditions. What is the reasonable thing to do in such circumstances? One view would have you make a marginal change to your immediate situation (put on additional clothing, seek temporary shelter etc.) and head on for the top. Alas many do not live to tell the tale of their adventures when using such decision rules, as a walk around the cemetery in Zermatt at the foot of the Matterhorn will quickly confirm. The golden rule of mountaineering in conditions of weather deterioration is to descend, however high up you are. Survival is the guiding principle. Live to climb another day. Some risks are just not quantifiable nor worth taking.

Investment under uncertainty also requires such 'survival' mechanisms. The pilot of the plane, the mountaineer and the fund-manager can all encounter similar problems! For all these individuals the secret of medium term success is to ensure survival. As Phillip Keane, one of the better-known active managers in the UK has said 'while advantage can sometimes be taken of market volatility, there will be uncertain periods when it is best to stand aside'. If the fund manager can avoid even a reasonable proportion of the meltdowns that an index investor is by definition exposed to, he is putting himself in a strong position to be able to outperform that index. The real issue for the fund manager is how can he build an alarm system that can hope to warn him of impending financial disasters?

EARLY WARNING SYSTEMS AS AIDS TO SURVIVAL

While it is not necessary for a good Early Warning System (EWS) to be outrageously technical, it is certainly the case that those with substantial historical experience in their particular field of investment will best be able to judge what type of EWS is appropriate in their case. The essence of the inductive approach is that experience matters (yes, there is a case for hiring back old fund managers out of retirement!). For the growth-orientated stock picker, for example, the secret will be look for advanced signals of potential earnings disappointments, an issue that T. Rowe Price was always at pains to emphasise was important within his investment philosophy. For the top-down asset allocator, the issue will be what fundamental forces drive particular markets and then to observe carefully these forces for signs of strain. It is important to emphasise that there is no 'right' way to build an EWS and ultimately it is up to the individual's skill and experience to build in the correct variables and the appropriate critical warning levels which capture the complexity of the particular investment areas in which he has decided to specialise.

Before giving an example of both a bottom-up and top-down EWS, we need to be clear on two issues which create inherent difficulties in building any EWS. Firstly, an EWS is unlikely to be one hundred per cent accurate, as we have already seen in the aviation case. Occasionally a false signal will be picked up. But 'lack of perfection' does not mean 'not useful' as the aeroplane example shows. The key issue is keeping false signals to a minimum. What one has to guard against obviously in any EWS is the danger of overkill. An EWS will be not particularly useful or comfortable in an aeroplane if it goes off every five minutes. Similarly with an EWS in financial markets.

The second issue relates to timing. In principle an EWS can alert to danger either too early or too late. In financial markets, it is not much use being alerted to a potential market collapse five years down the road, if in the meantime the market will soar. On the other hand, to be alerted to the fact that at the opening of the stock market tomorrow, shares will dive 30% is a little late to do much about it, especially if you are managing an enormous portfolio and today's session of the market is already over. Hence an EWS, even if correct, needs to be fairly well tuned if it is to achieve its purpose.

Yet the above problems do not obviate the need for a serious EWS approach. In both the Latin American and Asian stock market crises in the 1990s, the alternative of refusing to recognise the danger signs seems ludicrous. In the case of Mexico, as late as December 1994, a matter of days before the crisis broke, President Bill Clinton was extolling the 'economic miracle' of the country as a paragon for the region; in the case of Asia, three months before the Korean debacle, the IMF published a report praising the local administration for continued impressive economic performance. Both Mexico and Korea subsequently needed \$50bn plus bail-outs. And you wonder why I am cynical about governments and their various agencies!

A Top-down Asset Allocation Survival Approach

With these preliminaries in mind, let me proceed to outline the principles on which I have built an EWS to help give investment advice in emerging markets. Bubbles and setbacks in emerging markets have been a relatively frequent phenomenon for as long as capital has been free to invest in these countries. Historically a failure by a sovereign nation to honour its bond obligations could have serious consequences—when Mexico defaulted in 1862, the result was an invasion by its creditors Spain, France and Britain! How times change—as we have mentioned above, when Mexico was in danger of default at the beginning of 1995, its creditors put together a \$50bn rescue package!

While the immediate cause of reversals, such as that experienced by Mexico in 1995, is nearly always a loss of investor confidence, the warning signs can usually be picked up in economic variables long before that. My own approach to building an EWS for emerging markets focuses on identifying two longer-term problems which can emerge in such markets. Not all that emerges in emerging markets is good! When these longer-term trends become sufficiently negative, the EWS triggers additional short-term sensors designed to pick up definite signs of trouble ahead. The extent of the danger is measured on a simple risk score basis, which is normalised on a scale from one to one hundred so that the dangers can be expressed in a simple way. There is nothing magical about such a model—I have seen alternative and perhaps superior models which remain wholly qualitative and need no numbers at all! For reference I have reproduced in Table 4.1 one alternative such system from the absolutely excellent analysis on both emerging and developed markets available from Lombard Street Research.

The first longer-term trend I monitor is the evolution of capitalism in the economy. The evolution of capitalism in a country or region can be more or less healthy. 'Directed' credit within a quasi-capitalist system can often lead to a conglomerate-dominated market structure with the private sector colluding with the government or its various quangos. This must be distinguished from an economy where industrialisation is allowed to proceed in a relatively decentralised way, with the allocation of resources left principally to market forces. While judgements on what is and what is not a healthy development of capitalism are inevitably qualitative, we shall see later on that a sober judgement on these issues gave important clues of problems that were emerging in the Far East long before the 1997 crisis took hold.

The second longer-term trend I analyse is the evolution of government policy making in the economy. Too often governments embark on 'mission impossible', setting mutually-inconsistent and ultimately destructive targets. In particular, from economic theory we know that of the three objectives—a fixed exchange rate, free capital mobility, and an independent monetary policy—any two in combination, but not the three together are possible. For example, with free capital mobility and a fixed exchange rate, a country cannot simultaneously run an independent monetary policy. Why not? The very fact of fixing the exchange rate implies a commitment on behalf of the monetary authorities

Table 4.1 A Qualitative Early Warning System

	Philippines	*Indonesia*	*Thailand*	*Taiwan*
Big Debts	Y	Y	N	N
LT Inflows	Y	Y	Y	N
Large Portfolio Inflows	N	N	Y	N
Big ST Inflows	N	N	Y	N
Low Reserves	Y	Y	N	N
Fast M3 Growth	Y	Y	N	N
Fast GDP Growth	Y	Y	Y	Y
High Real Exchange Rate	Y	N	N	N
Big Current Acc Deficit	Y	Y	Y	N
Falling Investment	N	Y	N	N
Falling Savings	Y	Y	N	Y
Big Govt. Deficit	Y	N	N	Y
Bubble Stock Market	Y	Y	Y	Y
Score	***10***	***9***	***6***	***4***

Y = Yes; N = No.

Source: Brian Reading, Lombard Street Research Ltd. International Monthly Review No 36. Reproduced by permission.

in the country to issue domestic currency in exchange for foreign exchange reserves (or alternatively to buy domestic currency and run down its reserves of foreign currency) as demanded by the market. Thus the independence of domestic monetary policy in the sense of controlling the issue of base currency is lost.

Despite this compelling logic, many countries seem determined to defy the laws of economics. One should never underestimate the ability of politicians to embark on projects that defy all reason. Where a government is hell-bent on defying gravity in this way, such as was the case of Mexico, South Korea, Thailand, Malaysia and Indonesia this decade, I bring a further set of short-term indicators into the EWS. Why? The answer is simply because in these circumstances there is a much greater danger that capital flows into the country will ultimately prove to be damaging to financial market stability.

It might be thought by the novice that capital inflows to a country are unreservedly positive as it means that money is coming into the country. However, the fact is that capital inflows can be both potentially stabilising and destabilising in much the same way that borrowing by an individual may or may not be a good thing. On the positive side, capital inflows into a country can potentially finance investment that could otherwise not be afforded by the country and thus potentially increase the medium-term capital stock and growth prospects for the recipient country. However, capital inflows can be extremely dangerous in certain other circumstances, and particularly as we have said when capitalism is developing in a lop-sided way with too much state intervention, and/or when government policy objectives are inconsistent. Then one needs to watch the nature of capital flows with extreme care and in particular, the EWS system I use monitors the following:

The magnitude of capital flows relative to the size of the economy

This in itself is a measure of vulnerability of a developing economy—the larger the inflows the less likely it is that the economy can absorb the inflows without causing problems. The rate at which an economy's capital stock of private-sector factories and machinery on the one hand, and its stock of public goods such as roads and railways on the other, can be built up through investment is constrained by the overall flexibility of the economy to react to such investment. Normally bottlenecks and lags are the rule. However private and public consumption are easily expandable which is just what one might expect to happen when portfolio as opposed to direct inflows lead to surging equity markets and generate instant wealth as easily as instant coffee! A rule of thumb is that a repeated inflow year after year of 5% of GDP is unlikely to be sustainable in the medium-term. Certainly a repeated inflow of 10% of GDP as in Malaysia and Thailand in the 1990s was a clear sign of trouble ahead given a background of substantial government intervention in credit markets and inconsistent policy objectives.

The evolution of the overall current deficit is another way of inferring whether the size of capital inflows is potentially destabilising. By definition a private (or public) capital inflow must be matched either by an equal official outflow (purchase of foreign currency by the Central Bank) or by a current account deficit. Although it is possible to estimate more sophisticated rules on the sustainability of a current account deficit (see Table 4.2 for such an example), another simple rule of thumb is that a repeated current account deficit of over 3% of GDP is unlikely to be sustainable in the medium-term. Again deficits of 5–8% of GDP as in Mexico's case in the 1990s when growth is only 3% or less was another clear sign of problems ahead.

Table 4.2 Sustainability of Current Account Deficits (% GDP)

		Long Run GDP Growth (%)		
		2	4	6
Debt/GDP (%)	25	0.5	1.0	1.5
	50	1.0	2.0	2.5
	100	2.0	4.0	5.0

The table shows sustainable current account deficits for different levels of debt, relative to GDP, that foreign investors are prepared to hold. For example, if they are prepared to hold debt amounting to 100% of GDP, and the long-run growth is 2%, the country can sustain a 2% current account deficit relative to GDP.

Source: Sebastian Edwards, *Crisis and Reform in Latin America.*

The composition of capital flows

As we have already inferred, the split between short-term portfolio and long-term direct investment flows is a pointer to the likely resilience of the economy to any reversal in flows. Unfortunately it is particularly difficult to estimate what proportion of portfolio flows are long term and what proportion are short term in nature (unless the recipient nation defaults—then they are all long term!). Obviously funds invested in short term debt instruments tend to be extremely footloose, but even equity-related flows are often driven in and out of countries more on sentiment than anything else, and can easily generate asset bubbles and crashes in underdeveloped capital markets. What we can safely say is that the vast proportion of portfolio flows are potentially transitory while direct investment is much less so. Indeed, direct investment is in principle self-stabilising through a counterbalancing deterioration in the trade balance (as the recipient country imports capital goods to build and equip its new factories etc.).

The unravelling of the policy inconsistency

For a country exposed to capital flow shocks, in broad terms the issue is that government policy must not exacerbate structural tensions caused by the shock. That unfortunately is just what is happening if a country is simultaneously pursuing the three inconsistent objectives already discussed. How will the tension show itself up? Most likely one will see a build up of excessive foreign exchange reserves as a means to prevent the domestic nominal exchange rate from rising—when such reserves exceed around the value of nine months' imports, there is another signal that capital inflows are becoming potentially excessive. The build up of reserves will inevitably lead to a rising real exchange rate as domestic inflation rises, in the absence of the exchange rate being allowed to rise to a market-determined level. Overvalued and rising real exchange rates mean capital inflows are distorting price signals between the non-traded and traded goods sectors, potentially confusing the very export that free-trade policies are designed to encourage in domestic industry.

If domestic economic growth is strong, the party can go on for some time, with an ever-widening current account deficit emerging, normally increasingly funded by short-term inflows; when confidence is eventually shaken, short-term capital flows dry up overnight, but the real economy cannot adjust anywhere near as fast. At that stage it is the three Ds situation for the domestic government —devalue (hit foreign investors hard); deflate (hit domestic industry hard) or default (hit everyone hard). Apart from that, there is nothing that can be done, unless that is the Prime Minister is on friendly terms with the IMF in which case we have the fourth and fifth Ds—deflect the problem onto someone else and defer it for another day.

Using the above principles as a guide, I have for many years followed the global emerging markets, looking for warning signs of danger. For each of the potential danger variables, I track its behaviour and of related indicators over time, and when these move further and further from my estimate of an equilibrium or fair value, I have a simple 'barometer' which increases the 'danger score' for that country. Interestingly the barometer clearly signalled trouble ahead in Mexico as early as June 1994 (Figure 4.2).

By that time capitalism in Mexico was evolving in a dangerous way with a dominant party-political structure having a heavy influence on the allocation of credit. There was clear evidence of mounting political tensions (various assassinations including that of a Presidential candidate), and social tensions in parts of the country. Indeed, the astute fund manager from the Montgomery emerging markets fund, Josephine Jimenez, had visited Chiapas a year before the final financial crisis and could see the problems

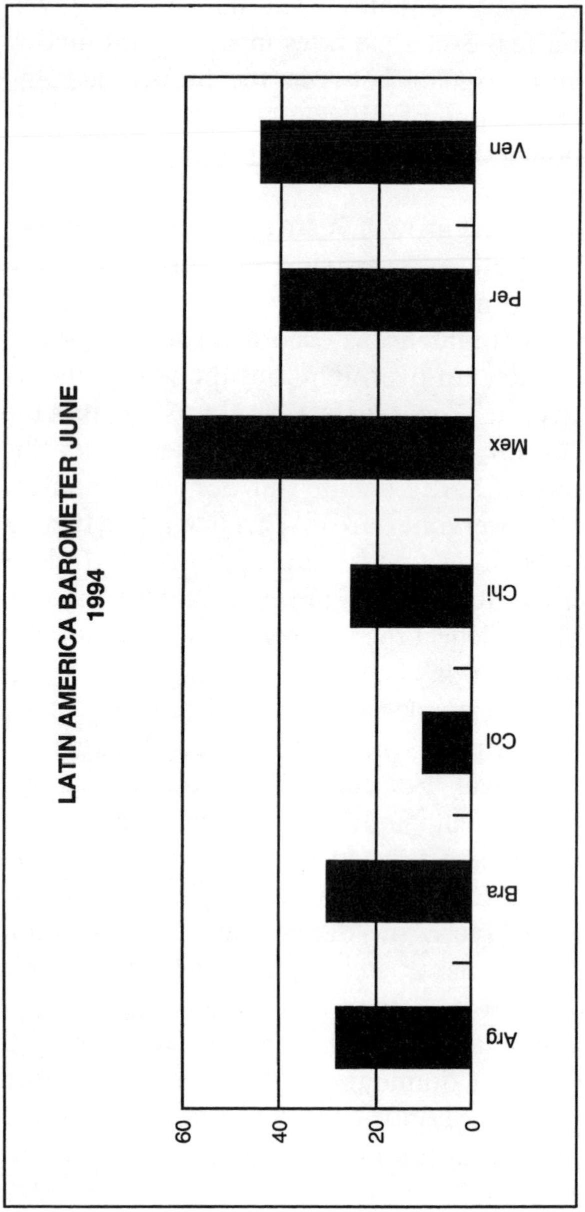

Figure 4.2 Early Warning Systems: The Mexico Case

mounting—she at least got her money out. The government was attempting to pursue the impossible policy triad of a steady exchange rate, free capital flows, but domestic monetary autonomy. The country was already a big debtor and a big borrower, with large short-term and very large portfolio inflows. An overvalued exchange rate had led to an unsustainable current account deficit, given low growth prospects and positive real interest rates. Capital inflows were being wasted on a higher consumption share of GDP rather than increased investment. The subsequent December crisis was an accident waiting to happen—and an accident that investors had the opportunity to avoid, and Bill Clinton would have had the opportunity to see, had they been using an EWS.

In the case of the Asian crisis of 1997, a related but distinguishable set of forces was at play, further proof, if proof be needed that in a complex financial world, the need to adapt one's hypotheses and vision is paramount to the investment process. Unlike most of Latin America where savings rates are generally low and foreign capital at least has the potential to speed up development, most of the Asian 'tigers' were high saving and high investing economies. Before the crisis hit the region in 1997, Thailand and Indonesia had investment rates exceeding 40% of GDP with Korea and Malaysia not far behind. All these countries had national savings rates of over 30%.

In one sense what was going on in Asia was no different from the case of Mexico—capitalism was developing in an unbalanced way and governments seemed determined to follow inconsistent sets of policies. However, in another sense, what was going on in Asia was rather different. Private capital flows are attracted to where risk-adjusted returns are perceived to be highest. Alan Greenspan, chairman of the US Federal Reserve, aptly described the problem shortly after the Asian crisis as a 'huge misallocation of resources' caused by an inflow of foreign capital from the world's financial centres failing to find 'adequate profitable opportunities at reasonable risk'. Perversely, 'well-perceived' emerging economies (which Asia traditionally had been, at least pre-crisis), which get glowing reports from the IMF and other supposedly august bodies may well attract excess capital which sets in train a set of adjustment mechanisms (rising reserves and real exchange rates, expanding current account deficits etc.) which will eventually lead to a denouement similar to capital reversals seen from economies lacking such apparently good credentials. Not only does the IMF shine the torch of moral hazard, it also makes it easy for you to play the game with its effective marketing!

The true lessons to be learned from the Asian crisis can probably best be understood by comparing within an EWS framework what were historically considered the region's identical twins, South Korea and Taiwan. Despite their apparent similarities and 'tiger' status, the response of the two economies to the crisis could hardly be more different. Korea's growth fell in 1997 to just 1%; the currency plummeted a staggering 80% over Q4 alone 1997 and the stock market moved in sympathy, falling 42% over the same quarter. Taiwan, on the other hand, saw growth of 6% in 1997 despite the crisis; the currency fell a modest 12% over Q4 1997, when the crisis was at its height, and the Taiwanese stockmarket actually rose over 1997 as a whole (see Figure 4.3). What was going on?

Both short-term and longer-term factors were at play. Short-term indicators clearly revealed differences between the two economies. Taiwan's investment rate was much more modest and sustainable than that in Korea (20% of GDP versus 40%), and its reliance on foreign savings amounted to a mere 10% of total investment since the 1960s, versus 60% in Korea. Investment was much more of the direct variety in Taiwan, and much more of the footloose portfolio variety in Korea—manufacturing debt/equity ratios in Taiwan pre-crisis were well under 100% but a massive 300% in Korea, and overall foreign debt in Taiwan was a mere \$100m versus an enormous \$250 bn in Korea.

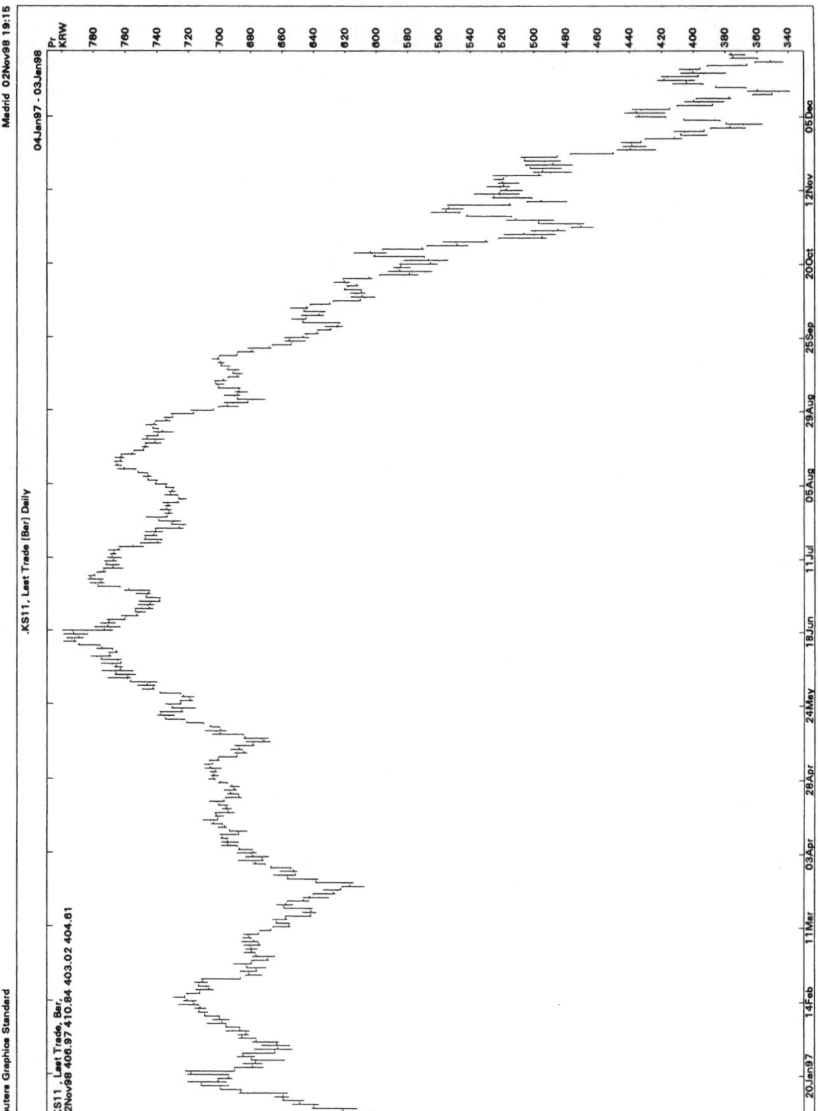
Reuters Graphics Standard
.KS11, Last Trade (Bar) Daily
Madrid 02Nov98 19:15
04Jan97 - 03Jan98
.KS11 , Last Trade, Bar,
02Nov98 406.97 410.84 403.02 404.61
Pr
KRW
780
760
740
720
700
680
660
640
620
600
580
560
540
520
500
480
460
440
420
400
380
360
340
20Jan97
14Feb
11Mar
03Apr
28Apr
24May
18Jun
11Jul
05Aug
29Aug
25Sep
20Oct
12Nov
05Dec

Figure 4.3a

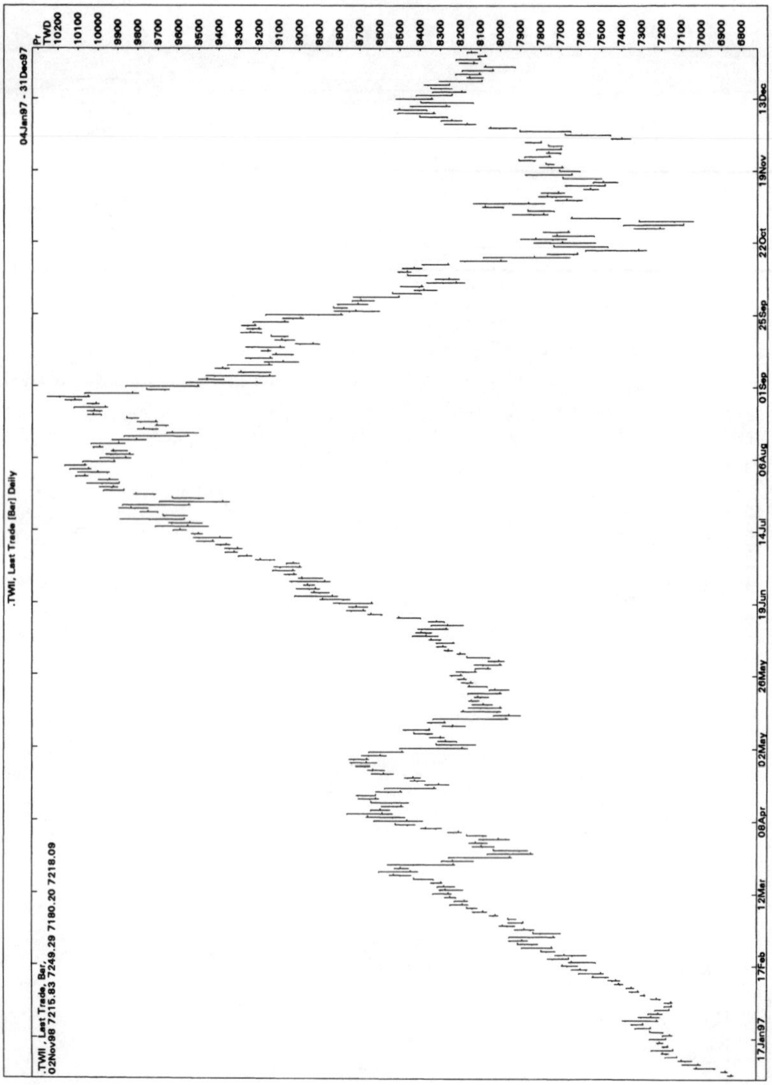

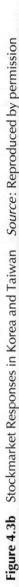

Figure 4.3b Stockmarket Responses in Korea and Taiwan *Source*: Reproduced by permission

Longer-term trends were also at work. In Taiwan, industrialisation had proceeded largely on a decentralised basis, with the economy dominated by small and medium-sized firms where the threat of bankruptcy was real if inefficiencies prevailed. In Korea, by contrast, the industrial model was one of the oligopolistic chaebols (conglomerates) dominating the economy thanks to government-directed and implicitly government-guaranteed bank loans.

Ultimately the lesson to be learned from the Asian crisis is again that there were parts of the region where an accident was one day inevitable. Yet proper analysis in the form of an EWS was sadly lacking and masked behind images of invincibility such as 'tiger economies'. When reality finally dawned and the self-fulfilling withdrawal of capital flows got going in earnest, the so-called tigers were quickly tamed.

A Bottom-up Stock Picking Survival Approach

Survival mechanisms are not solely the domain of the asset allocator, nor indeed that of the investor in emerging markets. Terry Smith, a leading UK company analyst and formerly head of UK company research at UBS Phillips and Drew, emphasises the need to strip away the camouflage entwined in company accounts even in developed countries if the investor is to make serious headway in stock picking. In his book *Accounting for Growth* Smith lists six survival techniques for the stock picker. By carefully compiling a health check list built around these techniques, Smith has consistently been able to identify corporate terminal cases, or if not substantial stock market underperformers. Amongst his techniques are:

1. Read the accounts backwards—remember that what the company is obliged by law to disclose but what it does not wish to draw attention to will more likely be found in the small print than in the Chair-

man's address. Far too many companies' annual reports reflect the skill of the company's public relations department rather than addressing the issues that are of serious interest to shareholders.

2. Generally beware of the auditor's report—many companies have gone bust despite an unqualified auditor's report. The auditor's report is no more than an opinion, and like all opinions, is fallible.
3. Screen accounts using your own filters. Here is just one to give a flavour of what sort of filters will be useful. Check the net interest income/interest expense ratio with the net cash/debt ratio. Are the two compatible? If not, perhaps there is a reasonable explanation such as seasonal factors but equally perhaps the reason is creative accounting.
4. Beware of companies that use accounting techniques to support the Profit and Loss account at the expense of the balance sheet. The obvious example is the capitalisation of costs where the analyst must satisfy himself that the procedure is appropriate—it may be quite reasonable for a property company to capitalise costs during a development phase in a property bull market; it may however be financial madness to capitalise development costs at the top of the market.
5. Compute a careful cash flow analysis adjusting the standard definition (net profit plus cash flow) for capital expenditure (should be deducted from cash flow as it represents a cash outlay on fixed assets) and adjusting for changes in working capital (if working capital requirements increase faster than profits, there will be a cash outflow from the business).
6. Finally, if in doubt, do not invest. Thus Smith has his own ultimate sanction or survival principle built into his investment philosophy.

My own stock analysis also follows a different but related

approach to 'weeding out' bad companies. The real value of a company is measured by the currency of its economic profit and not by the history of its accounts. For this reason, I prefer to attempt to calculate whether the existing assets in a business are, or are not, in true economic profit or loss. This involves calculating whether the business is generating sufficient operating free cash flow to cover its capital costs, including both a cost of debt and a cost of equity (see Box 4.3 for further details). To my mind, companies that fail this test are simply bad businesses which, unless there is sufficient evidence that the dynamics of the company are rapidly moving from bad to good, the investor should completely avoid.

And of course one should be careful with this type of analysis. Just because a business passes this test does not at all automatically mean it should be included in a portfolio.

Box 4.3 Filter Mechanisms in Stock Selection

A starting point for analysing whether or not a company is truly creating economic value is to consider the statement of Benjamin Graham whom we first met in Chapter 1. 'One cannot determine income or earnings unless one also determines that the original capital has been maintained.' To Graham's observation it should be added that, having conducted this exercise, one cannot assess whether those assets have generated a true economic profit without ensuring that a proper opportunity cost charge is attributed to the tax-adjusted cash earnings stream attributable to those assets.

To achieve this second objective, different authors have their own preferred methods. Two common starting points are either the company's Earnings before Depreciation, Interest and Tax (EBITDA) or its Earnings before Interest and Tax). I prefer the former since it explicitly considers the earnings generating power of the company's existing assets, rather than the latter which implicitly is mixing the earnings power of its existing assets with that of the new investment being undertaken (to which the depreciation charge will be linked). From EBITDA the major adjustment one needs to make to meet Graham's point is to subtract a charge which should reflect the cash capital expenditure necessary to maintain the existing assets (technically other minor adjustments should be made which need not concern us). The resulting figure measures the true operating cash flow of the company's existing assets. There are three claims on this income, those of government, debt holders and shareholders. Imputing a tax charge satisfies the former claim. Subtracting interest expenses rewards debt holders for their investment. But a further adjustment needs to be made to reflect the opportunity cost of equity capital tied up in the business. Unfortunately, the cost of equity capital is uncertain, in fact as uncertain as the uncertainty inherent in equity markets themselves! In practice, an estimate has to be made on a company by company basis—only after such a charge is imputed to earnings are we left with a measure, albeit imperfect, of economic profit.

An analysis over time of how this economic profit is evolving gives important clues to a company's longer-term viability. If it is going from bad to worse, then my investment advice would be to simply exclude such companies from a portfolio, in much the same way that Smith (see main text) has his ultimate sanction on companies where the uncertainties seem excessive. If these shares are 'cheap', they are cheap for a reason, and they are likely to stay cheap or get cheaper! In fact, investing in shares that are 'cheap' on any standard valuation basis such as the P/E ratio is in my experience about as effective an investment strategy as buying those on a high P/E ratio, an observation that not just ties in with my own experience but been confirmed by various rigorous studies of the US and other major markets over time! That says something not just about buying shares that are cheap, but also something about the value of the P/E ratio as an investment tool!

Orange County would have passed the above test marvellously for many years—in a single bad year it went bust! Whether one adopts a Smith-based approach to the survival principle, or the method outlined above, or indeed better still develops one for oneself, the basic point is that filter mechanisms have an important role to play in both asset allocation and stock selection processes in a complex world.

DEALING WITH COMPLEXITY—OTHER FILTERS

By its very nature, an inductive approach relies on individual experience to develop tentative rules to guide conduct. As the great investor Paul Cabot (the adviser who ran Harvard's endowment for seventeen years) was at pains to emphasise, there is no way to be a realist unless you have substantial experience of the many facets of reality, which in practice means having attained a certain age. The best advice to give is to read and re-read the experiences of some of the great investors of our time. They are a like a gold mine of knowledge on which the less-practised investor can draw as he discovers and deals with the complexities of the financial world for himself. What follows are a set of six provisional rules of thumb I use myself to guide me through the complexities of the investment world that I think should stand you in good stead—they have certainly proved robust in my own experience. They are filters designed to help deal with the uncertainties that ultimately make investment so difficult.

1. Beware of Excessive Diversification!

> 'Anyone owning such numbers of securities (100s) is what I call the Noah's ark school of investing—two of everything. Such investors should be piloting arks'.
>
> *Warren Buffett.*

So far we have argued that there is a strong case for both asset allocators and stockpickers to be prepared to ignore certain markets or stocks altogether if uncertainties and dangers are sufficiently high. But outside that, what should the investor do in a complex world? Do EWS systems, formal or informal, merely lead to a revised CAPM approach with significant diversification remaining after one has avoided the real basket-cases? I believe not. The principle is to invest, not to guess or to be just be following the crowd.

The fact is that diversification *à la* CAPM is mimicking the average. That is not to say that some diversification is not sensible, but rather that it should be concentrated in what you understand and can follow carefully. For a private investor there is a strong case for developing an interest and investing part of one's wealth in relatively unrelated asset classes to equities such as antiques, or paintings, to maximise the possible benefits from limited diversification. Of course for most institutional fund managers flexibility will not exist for such lavish diversification, but the principle must be that, whatever the investment constraints, it makes sense to differentiate investments as much as possible within the constraint of what one knows at least tolerably well.

But it is worth emphasising that differentiation does not imply massive diversification. We know from Chapter 2 that the major gains from diversification can be obtained by holding a relatively concentrated portfolio, consisting of as little as ten assets. In view of this, it seems much better to concentrate on knowing a few companies well, rather than diluting one's time and knowledge with unwieldy and poorly-understood portfolios.

A good rule of thumb for improving your investment performance is to perform a version of the Odysseus fable discussed in Chapter 3. The idea is to deliberately bind yourself to making only a limited set of new investments over a given time period, rather than investing in every apparently good idea that comes along. Deliberately avoiding some good ideas may seem less than fully rational, but remember it is the best ideas that you want. You only have to do a few things right, so long as you do not do too many things wrong. Hopefully a robust early warning system will avoid the latter pitfall, leaving the way clear to follow the former maxim. This is sometimes summed up as saying to follow the strategy of the hedgehog rather than that of the fox. The fox knows many little things; but the hedgehog knows one big thing. One of the ways to deal best with the complexities of uncertainty is to ration your limited intellectual resources to an extremely focused strategy.

2. Watch for Potential Biases in Yourself and in Other Investors!

> 'We have established that there is a lack of correspondence between the participant's thinking and the situation to which it relates'.
>
> *George Soros.*

What does cognitive psychology tell us about our ability to make judgements in complex situations? The full answer would run to a book in itself, but some idea of the issues involved can be gained through a look at the pioneering work in this area by Professors Daniel Kahnman and Amos Tversky. Both are veterans of strategy and well suited to examining this issue, having served in the Israeli armed forces during the 1950s. Over that time Kahnman developed a psychological screening system for new recruits that is still in use; Tversky served as a paratroops captain and earned a citation for bravery. Let us look at one particular bias and one particular inconsistency examined by these authors and by other psychologists which have particular relevance to financial markets.

First the bias. What Kahnman and Tversky refer to as the availability bias is our tendency to estimate probabilities using the most accessible information in our memory rather than considering a fuller information set. A classic example is the well-documented effect that immediately after a major earthquake or aeroplane disaster, there is a sharp increase in the purchase of earthquake or travel insurance but that the purchase rate soon drops back to 'normal' when the disaster ceases to be a recent event. More generally in financial markets, our estimates of whether prices are likely to appreciate or depreciate may be affected by the most recent changes in stock market prices; yesterday's price change tends to stand out in our memory and, as a result, disproportionately influences our estimate of future price changes. At an even more general level, we can see how this reasoning suggests that price appreciations or declines can be significantly influenced by the ease with which we can retrieve bullish or bearish information from our short-term memory bank. Hence vivid coverage by the media and pronouncements by respected 'gurus' can easily but unjustifiably alter our subjective estimates of potential future price changes. When making an investment decision, it is essential to put those 'players and painted stage' well out of mind. The objective must be to establish what the prospects are for any given investment, as far as possible, despite the uncertainties and complexities. Ultimately uncertainties may dictate that such judgements have to be qualitative rather than anything else, but even with qualitative judgements, the secret is to be ice-cold in analysis.

Secondly the inconsistency. From Chapter 1 we already realise that most people are risk averse, preferring the sure thing of a fixed sum of money to a gamble having the same expected value. Hence \$10 is preferred to the 50: 50 chance of either \$20 or \$0. But when confronted with the mirror image problem—a sure loss of \$10 or a 50: 50 chance of a loss of either \$20 or \$0, many 'risk averse' investors inconsistently and suddenly become 'risk lovers', preferring the gamble over the certain loss.

This type of behaviour has major implications for portfolio and stock selection. Consider the situation of an investor who is considering selling a stock that has already gone up. He faces the choice between selling and hence realising a certain gain, or holding the stock and realising either a further gain or being subjected to a loss of part of his gain. Similarly an investor who is considering selling a stock that has gone down faces the prospect of realising either a certain loss, or holding on to the stock and facing either a further loss or of recovering some of his money. The parallel with the abstract example in the previous paragraph is clear and may explain the noted tendency of some investors to sell their winners and hold on or increase their exposure to their losers through averaging down. Averaging down strategies should be avoided in the vast majority of cases, as should the temptation to sell once initial target prices have been reached. In a study of this phenomenon conduced by Srully Blotnick with more than one thousand investors over a period of ten years, he noted that an investor was over twenty times more likely to hold on to a stock all the way down than to fly with it all the way up.

Of course not only do we need to try to avoid these pitfalls in ourselves, but we also need to be aware that investors must to some degree be psychologists of other investors, and we must be prepared to contemplate in our own decision-making that other investors may at times be 'irrational' and prone to biases or inconsistencies such as those examined above. That in turn may mean that rationality may require us to temporarily assume a cloak of madness (think back to Odysseus in Chapter 2 and how he tried to avoid military service!). A classic example is the Soros description of the conglomerate boom in the 1960s and the real estate investment trust boom of the 1970s. In each case, while Soros realised the boom was ultimately unsustainable, the key to his success was not to counter the wave of irrational enthusiasm about conglomerates and real estate stocks but rather to ride the wave of excitement and sell out much later.

Of course, embarking on such a strategic course of action is not without its risks and can only be attempted by those with substantial experience such as Soros. A less fortunate example relates back to our South Sea Bubble described in Chapter 3 where Issac Newton's attempt to imitate madness cost him his whole investment!

As another example, consider an investor who had sold stocks immediately after Alan Greenspan's famous 'irrational exuberance' speech in December 1996. Greenspan's point was that, by late 1996, stocks were looking expensive given real earnings growth prospects. Be that as it may, a prevailing bias was driving stocks higher despite the warnings of the Fed chairman. In fact by the time of the general reversal of markets suffered in July 1998, the US market was almost 60% higher and the UK market over 50% higher. The German market rose more than 100% over that same period. Even after the sell-off and as this book is going to press, the US market is still some 40% up from the date of Greenspan's speech, the UK market 20% and Germany 50%! An investor who had sold out on Greenspan's initial warning would by now be in a different profession. When a prevailing bias is strong, it does not pay to go against it too early.

3. Beware of Simplistic Valuation Arguments!

> 'The combination of precise formulas with highly imprecise assumptions can be used to establish, or rather to justify, practically any value one wishes'.
>
> *Benjamin Graham.*

Any mathematical approach to valuation which concentrates on future earnings or growth prospects of companies potentially suffers from the so-called GIGO (garbage in garbage out) phenomenon. Brokers notes are full of increasingly technical arguments about valuation, but the fact is that a closer look at most valuation methods reveals that the estimated fair valuation of a stock is very susceptible to even small changes in assumptions. Growth estimates of sales and costs are diabolically difficult to estimate with any real accuracy over the medium term.

It is perfectly normal for a 1% change in the weighted average cost of capital used to discount a company's cash flows to imply a 20% or more change in estimated fair value for a stock. And given that the weighted average cost of capital includes the unobservable cost of equity, which itself encapsulates the so-called 'risk' premium of the company's equity (better called uncertainty premium!?) about which wide variations of opinion are inevitable, substantial care is required in interpreting mathematical estimates of fair value. As an example, Table 4.3 shows a variety of fair values for the Spanish motorway stock Aumar constructed by my

Table 4.3 The Sensitivity of Fair Values to Assumptions

		Traffic Increase (%)							
	Target Price (Pts)	0	4	8	16	21	22	24	26
	3.00%	3900	4185	4470	5040	5395	5470	5610	5750
	3.25%	3750	4030	4305	4855	5200	5275	5410	5550
	3.50%	3610	3880	4145	4685	5020	5085	5220	5355
	3.75%	3470	3735	3990	4520	4845	4910	5040	5170
	4.00%	3345	3600	3855	4360	4680	4745	4870	4995
	4.25%	3225	3470	3720	4210	4520	4580	4705	4830
Bond	4.50%	3100	3345	3585	4065	4365	4425	4545	4665
Yield	4.75%	2990	3230	3460	3930	4220	4280	4395	4510
	5.00%	2885	3115	3340	3795	4080	4135	4250	4365
	5.25%	2780	3005	3225	3670	3945	4000	4110	4220
	5.50%	2685	2900	3120	3550	3815	3870	3980	4085
	5.75%	2590	2800	3015	3433	3695	3745	3850	3955
	6.00%	2500	2710	2913	3320	3575	3630	3730	3830
	6.25%	2420	2615	2817	3215	3465	3515	3615	3715
	6.50%	2335	2530	2725	3115	3355	3405	3500	3600

research colleague Ricardo Morales, contingent on different estimates about plausible levels of traffic growth and the appropriate discount rate. The range of fair values is enormous.

4. Be Creative!

> 'I did not play the financial markets according to a particular set of rules; I was always more interested in understanding the changes that occur in the rules of the game'.
>
> *George Soros.*

One must never lose a sense of creativity in how to look at financial markets and individual companies—not everything is simply a re-run of what has happened before. The accomplished investor will always look to pick up signs of change, which can take many shapes and forms, including when fashions in the investment community are moving towards particular markets or sectors, or when ways of valuation are being reviewed, and also including the more basic strategic changes that companies go through over their life cycle.

The heart of the message of this chapter is that in a complex world, no financial relationships are likely to remain for ever—all articles of faith come of age. From 1871–1958, stock yields in the US exceeded bond yields by an average of over 1 % every year, with only three transitory reversals. That lead to a general view that good US stocks had to yield more than bonds, and if they did not, a nasty price correction was on the way. No one dreamed of anything different. The relationship fell apart at the end of the fifties and since then, bond yields have exceeded stock yields on the US market by over 3% on average.

The advent of an inflationary world had taken its inevitable toll on what, historically, had been seen as a 'riskless' investment (government bonds). Yet what is interesting about this paradigm change is that the writing had been on the wall for some time. Between 1800 and 1940, inflation in the US had averaged only 0.2% per annum, a rate which puts any of today's hard currencies to shame. Yet from 1940 until 1959, inflation averaged 4% per year. Why was the change in structure in bond and equity yields so unexpected? The only credible answer is that investors, many of them veterans of the Great Crash of 1929, saw the yield change as another aberration that would quickly change with a fall in stock prices. What was required but was lacking was creativity and the vision of a new paradigm, which alas was blinded in many cases by a belief that nothing changes. Perhaps today, as a new millennium approaches, we again will need to rethink the relationship between bonds and equities as economies potentially return to a very low-inflation era, or even possibly deflation after the relatively high inflation era of the second half of the twentieth century.

Such potentially important changes also happen at the stock level. Yes, leopards do change their spots, at least in the financial world. Who would have thought that a little known forestry company that had nearly gone into bankruptcy in the 1980s as it diversified into everything from toilet paper to engineering, would be the largest mobile phone company in the world before the end of the century? Yet that is exactly what happened to Nokia, the Finnish telecommunications company that became the largest seller of mobile phones in the world, surpassing even the mighty Motorola, in 1998. The rules of the game do change!

5. Watch what the Big Investors are Doing

> 'Given two similar companies, one where there is no corporate potential because of the shareholder structure and one where there is, I'd always choose the one where there is corporate potential.'
>
> *Anthony Bolton.*

Most quoted companies will have large shareholders. This is especially true in Europe where substantial cross-shareholdings are common. Whatever the situation, in any company in which you are considering investing, either for yourself or for the fund you are managing, it pays to know exactly what the biggest shareholders in the company are up to. That can give you vital clues about future prospects for the company you are looking at. And keeping an eye on what the core shareholders are up to need not always be that boring as the following story hopefully will illustrate.

By the late 1980s in Spain it was becoming increasingly clear that the banking system was in need of a substantial restructuring. A cult of directed credit and State involvement in the sector had left some banks with poor loan books and others with sprawling industrial empires. Two such banks were Banesto (now part of the Santander Group) and Banco Central (now integrated in to BCH Group). In 1988, the then President of Banesto, Mario Conde, proposed a merger between the two groups that would have created Spain's largest bank at the time with assets of nearly $50 billion. The Kuwait Investment Office (KIO), already a holder of a five per cent stake in Central, saw the chance of huge restructuring potential from the merger of the two groups, together with numerous corporate opportunities (both banks had sizeable industrial holdings), and immediately piled into the market for both shares, aiming to become the leading shareholder in the merged group. Everything seemed set for a major increase in profitability at the two banks and the two shares reacted accordingly. Analysts pumped out research notes extolling the advantage of the merger for shareholders.

Seemed watertight? On the available numbers many would have been convinced of the investment case. The problem, however, lay with one of the major shareholders, the KIO. Their investments in the banking sector in Spain were conducted on a joint-venture basis with two cousins and prominent Spanish businessmen, Alberto Cortina and

Alberto Alcocer. The two cousins had come to particular fame through their marriage to two sisters, Alicia and Esther Koplowitz, themselves daughters of a wealthy Spanish marquesa who had died young, leaving the daughters in control of a large property, construction and investment company, now called FCC.

Anyway the problem was that the Albertos became a little unruly, not just in the boardroom but in the bedroom as well. KIO wanted the deal, but the cousins kept holding out for better terms, largely with a view to increasing their own influence post-merger. The KIO were not amused.

And then a strange thing happened. Alicia's husband Alberto Cortina slipped off to the Schwarzenburg Palace Hotel in Austria and was unlucky enough to be photographed emerging from the hotel with the glamorous Marta Chavarri. Just to show how much Marta liked to enjoy herself, the Spanish magazine *Interviu* promptly published a picture of her at a well-known night-club wearing an orange mini-skirt with nothing underneath except a pair of completely see-through tights! Divorce proceedings were instigated immediately by the unamused Alicia.

Who paid the photographer outside the hotel? We shall never know, but one view has it that the KIO set Alberto up, as a way to get rid of him. With all the bad publicity surrounding the infighting between the KIO and the Albertos, the shares of Banesto and Central had lost their sparkle on the market. Whatever the facts, the point is that to understand the movements of the Banesto and Central share prices over the period required an understanding of the infighting going on between some of the major shareholders. It also required careful reading of the gutter press a good deal more than the financial press!

On a more serious note, I am sure many investment mistakes made by fund managers happen through insufficient attention to the core shareholder base at companies. Often one can infer by observing these shareholders what plans are afoot, or what dangers are lurking. In fact Banesto itself was to prove the same point years later. After it narrowly avoided bankruptcy in 1994, a majority stake was acquired by the Banco Santander Group, but the minority remained in the stock market. By 1997, the share price of Banesto was well beyond anything that could be justified on the fundamentals. Some hedge funds went short, believing a correction to be well overdue. But the price stayed resolute. In 1998 Santander launched a knock-out bid for the outstanding equity. The hedge funds had underestimated the determination of Santander to strengthen its domestic presence.

6. Speculate!

> 'When it's easy to lose money you've got to survive. Why stand up to be machine gunned?
>
> *John Armitage.*

This might be the last thing you would expect as investment advice from this author. But I use the word carefully, in the sense of its Latin root 'speculae'—watch-towers that surrounded the great Roman cities and from which the army would hopefully perceive advanced warning of impending danger. And that brings me neatly back to the first theme of this chapter, the need for investors to develop robust early warning systems, whatever their particular investment expertise. I take this to be speculation as the word should be understood in finance. But speculation in this sense is exactly what CAPM will not let you do—with CAPM, as we stated in the introduction, you appear to go to bed and sleep easy at night. But do you really? Given an investment world as we have described it in Chapter 3, is it not better to leave someone on the watchtower as the twilight closes in?

As this book draws to a close, I hope by now to have said enough to show that passive portfolio indexing as a strategy lacks theoretical support and that alternative approaches exist which potentially seem more reasonable approaches to investment given the underlying complexities. I have tried to bring back the active fund manager from the wings, if not to the centre stage, then at least to a place where he potentially has a major role to play.

But ideas die hard! I can still see the convinced index investor coming back with a final argument. For the index investor, the theoretical case for his approach may have been weakened, but he can still fall back on an inductive argument to support his case—the practical inability of many fund managers to beat the index in a consistent way might be a simple empirical and practical argument in favour of a passive indexing approach, whatever the lack of rigorous theoretical underpinnings for the approach.

But now the argument has changed subtly but importantly. In effect this argument says not that you cannot beat the 'market' but that you cannot beat the 'crowd'. The problem with this position is that we can all think of situations where following the crowd can be the right thing to do, but equally many situations where it is simply the daft or dangerous thing to do. And even in those cases where following the crowd can be rational (trying to get one's money out of a bank that is rumoured to be going under; trying to get out of a cinema that is on fire through the emergency exit, etc.), it usually pays to be as near the front of the queue as possible. To my mind that is crucial—the failure of many to be no better than average is no excuse for accepting the average as the best one can achieve. That ultimately underlies the philosophy of all the great investors we mentioned in the introduction to this book. Ultimately the truly active investor realises the underlying difficulties, but must aim high. Why accept less? Speculate!

CONCLUDING COMMENTS—INVESTING IN THE TWILIGHT

It is time to bring together the various themes of this book.

First we need to be clear on one thing. This book is not 'anti-mathematical'; it is just that the mathematical tools and models finance theorists currently use to examine financial markets seem inadequate to capture the realities of financial markets. That proposition looks particularly evident when looking at CAPM. At one stage it was hoped that the mathematics associated with 'chaos' theory could take us further down the road to such understanding. However, the more this author thinks about that route, the less convinced he is of its relevance. Chaotic systems do not change and do not adapt, but adaptation is at the heart of what happens in financial systems where the actors on the stage affect the very structure of that same stage by their actions. I believe that such complexity is at best imperfectly understood at the present time, and that deductive models, while perhaps shining a spotlight on certain areas of importance, leave much left wholly in the darkness. Maybe the US banking group State Street's decision in late 1998 to patent a stock picking technique relying on neural networks holds an important mathematical key to future developments in finance—only time will tell. For the moment we are left in the twilight.

The twilight is on the edge of day and night, where the shadows only allow us to perceive certain things imperfectly while other things remain completely hidden from sight. It is traditionally a time of opportunity and excitement. But it is a time when our perceptions can easily deceive us. And it is also a time when danger lurks in the shadows, and when we must keep alert to avoid deadly pitfalls.

John Locke, one of Britain's great empiricists, used the image of the twilight to describe the human condition and the frailty of our knowledge. The image also serves clearly to describe the investment universe and our imperfect understanding of its complexity. Uncertainty in the context of the financial world is particularly devilish, and we cannot rely on the laws of probability to guide us, nor can we rely on some inevitability to dictate market behaviour. The uncertainty of financial markets is so diabolical because we ourselves make it that way, affecting through our various conjectures and actions the very outcomes we are trying to predict. The level of complexity involved will always leave many things unknown, 'black holes' in our knowledge that can easily trap the unwary.

As even the great Kenneth Arrow has said, alluding both to the great English poet Wordsworth and to the father of philosophy, Plato himself, 'our knowledge of the way things work, in society or in nature, comes trailing clouds of vagueness'. The shrewd investor must face up to this challenge, using inductive references as a guide through the vagueness. The only generalisations of much use when investing in the twilight are to do everything possible to avoid the worst pitfalls, to stick as far as possible to what one knows at least reasonably well, and to keep a creative spirit, constantly on the look-out for paradigm changes. Above all perhaps, a sense of humility is in order. I am reminded of a great comment by another outstanding investment professional, John Train:

> 'I do not have precise religious ideas, but I do observe that God is like this. He observes our proud manoeuvres here below and says to himself, or herself or itself—oh he thinks that does he? He says that does he?—Zap! Hubris really does lead to nemesis'

It seems fitting to end in these literary terms—when all is said and done, investment is as much art as science.

Bibliography

Anand, P. 1993. *Foundations of Rational Choice under Risk*. Oxford University Press.

Arrow, K. 1971. *Essays in the Theory of Risk Bearing*. Markham.

Begg, D. 1982. *The Rational Expectations Revolution in Macroeconomics*. Phillip Allan.

Bernstein, P. 1996. *Against the Gods*. New York: John Wiley and Sons.

Blotnick, S. 1979. *The Psychology of Successful Investing*. New York: McGraw-Hill.

Coddington, A. 1983. *Keynesian Economics, the Search for First Principles*. London: George Allen and Unwin.

Cohen, B. 1997. *The Edge of Chaos*. Chichester: John Wiley and Sons.

Copeland, T., Koller, T. and Murrin, J. 1990. *Valuation, Measuring and Managing the Value of Companies*. Chichester: John Wiley and Sons.

Corden, M. 1994. *Economic Policy, Exchange Rates and the International System*. Oxford University Press.

Cross, R. (ed.) 1988. *Unemployment, Hysteresis and the Natural Rate Hypothesis*. Oxford: Basil Blackwell.

Edwards, S. 1995. *Crisis and Reform in Latin America*. Oxford University Press.

Elster, J. 1984. *Ulysses and the Sirens*. Cambridge University Press.

Garcia Marquez, G. 1970. *One Hundred Years of Solitude*. London: Harper and Row.

Hargreaves Heap, S. and Y. Varoufakis. 1995. *Game Theory*. London: Routledge.

Hicks, J. 1967. *Critical Essays in Monetary Theory*. Oxford University Press.

Hicks, J. 1974. *The Crisis in Keynesian Economics*. Oxford: Basil Blackwell.

Hirshleifer, J. 1992. *The Analytics of Uncertainty and Information*. Cambridge University Press.

Hume, D. 1777. *Enquiries Concerning Human Understanding and Concerning the Principles of Morals*, 3rd edn. Oxford University Press.

Jensen, M. (ed.) 1982. *Studies in the Theory of Capital Markets.* Westport, CT: Praeger.

Keynes, J.M. 1931. *Essays in Persuasion.* London: Macmillan.

Keynes, J.M. 1936. *The General Theory of Employment, Interest and Money.* Cambridge University Press.

Kindleberger, C. 1978. *Manias, Panics and Crashes.* New York: John Wiley and Sons.

Lofthouse, S. (ed.) 1994. *Readings in Investments.* Chichester: John Wiley and Sons.

Lowenstein, R. 1995. *Buffett: The Making of an American Capitalist.* London: Weidenfeld & Nicolson.

Markowitz, H. 1959. *Portfolio Selection.* Chichester: John Wiley and Sons.

McWhirter, L. 1977. *Astrology and Stock Market Forecasting.* New York: ASI Publishers.

Milne, F. 1995. *Finance Theory and Asset Pricing.* Oxford University Press.

Modigliani, F. and M. Miller. 1958. The cost of capital, corporation finance, and the theory of investment. *American Economic Review* (September).

Norton, J. 1997. *Investing with the Grand Masters.* FT Pitman Publishing.

von Neumann, J. and O. Morgenstern. 1944. *Theory of Games and Economic Behaviour.* Princeton University Press.

Nozick, R. 1993. *The Nature of Rationality.* Princeton University Press.

Oppenheimer, A. 1996. *Bordering on Chaos.* New York: Little, Brown and Co.

Rutherford, J. 1993. *Introduction to Stock Exchange Investment.* 2nd edn. London: Macmillan.

Sargent, T. 1993. *Bounded Rationality in Macroeconomics.* Oxford University Press.

Savage, L. 1954. *The Foundations of Statistics.* New York: John Wiley and Sons.

Schelling, T. 1963. *The Strategy of Conflict.* Harvard University Press.

Schelling, T. 1978. *Micromotives and Macrobehaviour.* New York: WW Norton and Co.

Sharpe, W. 1985. *Investments* Englewood Cliffs, NJ; Prentice Hall.

Smith, T. 1992. *Accounting for Growth.* New York: Century Business Books.

Soros, G. 1987. *The Alchemy of Finance.* New York: John Wiley and Sons.

Tobin, J. 1980. *Asset Accumulation and Economic Activity.* Oxford: Basil Blackwell.

Train, J. 1980. *The Money Masters.* London: HarperCollins.

Varian, H. 1994. *Microeconomic Analysis.* New York: WW Norton and Co.

Index

Index compiled by Geoffrey Jones